NO PLACE LIKE HOME

NO PLACE LIKE HOME

Enemy Alien Internment in Canada during the Great War

BOHDAN S. KORDAN

McGILL-QUEEN'S UNIVERSITY PRESS
Montreal & Kingston • London • Chicago

ISBN 978-0-2280-2467-5 (paper)
ISBN 978-0-2280-2530-6 (ePDF)
ISBN 978-0-2280-2531-3 (ePUB)

Legal deposit second quarter 2025
Bibliothèque et Archives nationales du Québec

Printed in Canada on acid-free paper that is 100% ancient-forest-free, containing 100% sustainable, recycled fibre, and processed chlorine-free.

This project has been made possible by a grant from the Endowment Council of the Canadian First World War Internment Recognition Fund as well as a St Thomas More College publishing subvention.

We acknowledge the support of the Canada Council for the Arts.
Nous remercions le Conseil des arts du Canada de son soutien.

Funded by the Government of Canada | Financé par le gouvernement du Canada | Canada

Canada Council for the Arts | Conseil des arts du Canada

McGill-Queen's University Press in Montreal is on land which long served as a site of meeting and exchange amongst Indigenous Peoples, including the Haudenosaunee and Anishinabeg nations. In Kingston it is situated on the territory of the Haudenosaunee and Anishinaabek. We acknowledge and thank the diverse Indigenous Peoples whose footsteps have marked these territories on which peoples of the world now gather.

LIBRARY AND ARCHIVES CANADA CATALOGUING IN PUBLICATION

Title: No place like home : enemy alien internment in Canada during the Great War / Bohdan S. Kordan.
Names: Kordan, Bohdan S., author
Description: Includes bibliographical references and index.
Identifiers: Canadiana (print) 20250114275 | Canadiana (ebook) 20250114291 | ISBN 9780228024675 (paper) | ISBN 9780228025313 (ePUB) | ISBN 9780228025306 (ePDF)
Subjects: LCSH: World War, 1914-1918—Prisoners and prisons, Canadian. | LCSH: Internment camps—Canada—History—20th century. | LCSH: Prisoners of war—Canada—History—20th century.
Classification: LCC D627.C2 K668 2025 | DDC 940.4/7271—dc23

This book was designed and typeset by Lara Minja in Dante MT Pro 11 pt/14 pt. Copyediting by Joanne Richardson.

McGill-Queen's University Press
Suite 1720, 1010 Sherbrooke St West, Montreal, QC, H3A 2R7

Authorized safety representative in the EU: Mare Nostrum Group BV, Mauritskade 21D, 1091 GC Amsterdam, the Netherlands, gpsr@mare-nostrum.co.uk

FOR MY PARENTS,
ANDRIJ AND FENNA,
WHO LOVED ME SO.

CONTENTS

ACKNOWLEDGMENTS

Writing is a laborious journey. Along the way we rely on others for assistance and support. This journey is no different. The contributions that helped realize this project have been both varied and significant. There are, as a result, many to thank and much to be thankful for.

The work in this volume appeared over the years in different venues as book chapters and articles. For permitting their use, I gratefully acknowledge the University of Toronto Press, Cornell University Press, Routledge, the *Journal of Canadian Studies*, *Canadian Military History*, *Ontario History*, and *Canadian Speeches: Issues of the Day*. I am also indebted to those with whom I worked in bringing some of these to light: Stefan Manz, Panikos Panayi, Matthew Stibbe, Rotem Kowner, Iris Rachaminov, Barry Wright, Eric Tucker, Susan Binnie, Geoffrey Hayes, Brittany Dunn, and Tory Tronrud. James Farney, a partner in writing, kindly agreed to have a co-authored essay appear in this collection, and to him I extend my heartfelt thanks

Throughout the years, the Prairie Centre for the Study of Ukrainian Heritage at St Thomas More College, University of Saskatchewan, supported me on this and many other projects. I count myself fortunate to have enjoyed the patronage of the centre. I also wish to acknowledge with thanks St Thomas More College, which generously contributed to the publication through its grants program. Production of the book was further supported by much-welcomed assistance from the Shevchenko Foundation and its First World War Internment Legacy Fund, an organization whose commitment to education, culture, and community has been outstanding. I am truly grateful for this support.

McGill-Queen's University Press has been my publisher of choice for these many years. This is because the staff has always been helpful and accommodating. But they are also committed to excellence, and the publications that appear under their watch are superb. They are simply the best. In particular, Jonathan Crago, MQUP's associate director and editor in chief, guided me through the vetting and editing process, for which I am greatly appreciative. The hidden magic behind any successful book is the copyediting. The magician in this instance is Joanne Richardson, whose skill is only matched by her talent. My thanks for helping to craft a much better manuscript.

In this, as in so many other projects, I have been sustained by my partner and the love of my life, Danya. Her kind heart and loving nature have made everything I do lighter and easier. For this and much more I am deeply thankful. My children, Christian and Meagan, have moved on, carving out a future together, helping others as physicians. Their love and respect, however, remain a constant. They nourish and give me comfort every day, and no words are sufficient to convey my immense sense of pride and joy.

I came to this subject by way of decades of study and teaching in the areas of conflict and diplomacy, nations and nationalism, minorities and rights. This has shaped my thinking. But the subject is also personal. My parents, Andrij and Fenna, fled their ancestral home, escaping the violence and calamity of an all-consuming war. They sought sanctuary and Canada provided a place of refuge. In Canada, they struggled to make a home for themselves and their children – my sister and myself. It is both fitting and right, therefore, that I dedicate this book to them – a book about home. With love and admiration for their courage, selflessness, and hard work, I am eternally grateful. They were and are my inspiration.

PREFACE

The following essays represent decades-long work on a subject that generally is neither well known nor sufficiently understood – First World War internment in Canada. These were written over an extended period for different purposes and diverse audiences. The majority appeared as publications in a range of venues; some still accessible, others not. Believing there was value in bringing them under a single cover, these were reworked and stitched together into a manageable and readable whole. Some repetition remains to preserve the structure and integrity of the original arguments; nevertheless, considerable effort has been made to reduce redundancy. The value of the essays is that, as discrete chapters, they offer historical and political insights into Canadian internment. However, they can also be read as an unabridged narrative and, thus, collectively serve both as a singular statement about immigrant belonging during a time of war and as a resource in the continuing effort to understand the experience.

Overall, this book represents an analytical take on First World War internment in Canada. The focus is on what happened and why, bringing attention to the issues of immigrant fit and belonging. But there is also the question of historical memory and the importance of remembering. There are compelling reasons to broaden our knowledge of internment and to recall what happened, not least of which is the political and moral imperative to ensure that this experience is never repeated. This work looks to achieve this by giving voice to the idea that the decision to intern, and the way it was implemented, represented a political choice that affected thousands of innocents who had made Canada their home. It is a perspective that should resonate with us today as a rights-bearing people and serves as a reminder to those who would lead this country. Just as good government was important then, so it is today – a consequence of the moral choices we make.

NO PLACE LIKE HOME

INTRODUCTION

The Trouble with Home

Canadian Internment during the Great War

At the start of the Great War, John Kondro, being without work or registration papers that identified him as an immigrant of enemy origin, was arrested and interned in Canada as a prisoner of war (POW). He was sent to a camp established for this purpose at the base of Castle Mountain, a majestic peak located in Canada's national Rocky Mountains Park. John's father, Jacob Kondro, sought to intervene. He argued that, as he was a naturalized citizen, so was his dependent son. Therefore, the boy could not have been an "enemy." Moreover, he declared the lad – who was seventeen years of age – had nothing to do with the war. The father pleaded for his son's release. His appeal, however, was ignored, even though internment officials privately conceded a "British subject" was likely behind barbed wire. Labouring under a punishing work schedule and anxiously awaiting his release – a parole that never came – the young Kondro eventually took matters into his own hands. Along with four associates, he escaped under a volley of gunfire, disappearing into the forest deep, forever lost to his family and friends.[1]

The narrative of First World War Canadian internment consists of many such stories – of pluck and survival, of endurance and misfortune – each unique. Yet the Kondro case also alludes to a phenomenon shared among those affected by internment: the problem of fit within Canadian society. Following an immigration policy designed to meet the requirements of a developing economy, families like the Kondros arrived in Canada at the turn of the century, inhabiting the role of agriculturalists and industrial labourers while struggling to make their way in the country.[2] But immigration policy also echoed the British imperial project, which, in keeping with the ethnic and racial biases underpinning its construction, sought to shape a model settler society.[3] Between these two priorities, there was limited scope for the Kondros to have agency except in terms set out by the dominant Anglo-majority.

With the onset of the global conflict, the issue of compatibility was magnified. As economic dislocation accompanied a society transitioning to war, and with unemployment intensifying, attention focused on a demographic that had previously a functional role to play but now, increasingly, was seen to have none. Meanwhile, as empires battled for supremacy and dominance, the cultural dissonance of being a stranger in a strange land assumed a more aspersive character.[4] So, with a diminishing economic role and as a proverbial "outsider," the migrant originating from lands at war with Canada was characterized in the context of war as not only being superfluous but also an enemy alien.

This reconceptualization of migrants as the enemy was a result of their tenuous relationship with Canada. This proved to be an important first step in the internment story because, for those without work, it held out the possibility of restoring their original economic function, albeit under entirely different circumstances. Under exceptional conditions, the international Hague convention governing the laws of war permitted the internment of civilians of enemy origin as POWs. The convention also allowed for war prisoners to be put to work.[5] Accordingly, John Kondro and others who were interned would work as POWs. For this to happen, however, it was necessary to craft the appropriate domestic political and legal frameworks.

To this end, the Royal Proclamation of 15 August 1914 identified migrants from Germany, Austria-Hungary, and other belligerent lands as enemy aliens. But it was Order-in-Council PC 2721, issued on 28 October under the War Measures Act, that sanctioned the internment of jobless enemy aliens as POWs for the purpose of having them work. Though the decrees were framed in the language of security, in fact, they were expressions of the mistrust and animus directed towards the enemy alien, giving shape to the role and meaning of internment.[6] It did not matter that John Kondro was a Canadian citizen. Without work and as a person of suspicion, he would be arrested, held indefinitely, and forced to labour as a POW.

Meanwhile, the elder Kondro found it inconceivable "that Canada would take their own people and put them in an internment camp."[7] Canada was his home, and as it had originally extended a welcoming invitation, Kondro's faith in the country was absolute. He expected fair treatment and the rule of law to apply, which led him to believe that his son's imprisonment was a mistake. What Jacob Kondro could not have foretold, however, was that the government deemed internment useful in addressing issues fomented by the presence of enemy aliens in the country. From the government's perspective, internment was a strategic move, the consequences of which could be navigated and even weathered.

As for the young John Kondro, internment proved unbearable. Subjected to an unforgiving regime of forced labour and abuse, he fled. Risking being shot, it was a risk worth taking since the arguments tendered by the prisoners – namely, that they were civilians and therefore innocent – appeared to fall on deaf ears. It was made clear to Kondro and others like him that their predicament was of little interest or concern to their overseers. Alone in their thoughts, was it any wonder that despair and dread coloured their vision of the future, making escape the only alternative? But to where? Was Canada not their home?

Home is the touchstone that connects the disparate elements of the internment story. Although thoughts of home are frequently associated with place of birth, in the national narrative that is Canada, where immigration has played a significant role, the idea of home is normally linked to questions of trust, faith, and norms of reciprocity while immigrant integration and settlement, central to the notion of home, are closely connected to acceptance and tolerance. At the start of the twentieth century, the grip exerted by the ideology of imperialism on both the Canadian polity and society thwarted the possibility of creating a haven called home. Imperialism was a political construct grounded in the language of power, its hold and influence contingent upon ensuring that racial hierarchies and social boundaries were maintained.[8] This meant, among other things, that the role of the immigrant would be limited.[9] What, then, are we to make of home as a place of sanctuary and longing? Was it realizable or simply an illusion? Did the politics of belonging get in the way?

In the lead-up to the Great War, the imperial idea held sway.[10] With global migration accelerating and immigrants an important economic resource, imperialism in Canada collided with the modern concept of the nation-state and nation-building process. By challenging alternative modes of belonging – through bonds of citizenship, for example – and by prioritizing duty to a sovereign over community, imperialism represented both a test and a choice regarding Canada's future. Choice, of course, presumes autonomy. But could Canada escape the legacy of empire?

Filtered through an imperial lens and the coming of war, the question of who belonged became more urgent and the tension around the issue became increasingly palpable. The need for security – a framework determining the parameters of fit – demanded a policy response.[11] Yet how was a comprehensive security to be attained when migrant workers, including those of enemy origin, were still needed? The Royal Proclamation issued at the start of the conflict looked to square the contradiction by stating that aliens of enemy nationality could go about their business freely if they abided by the laws of the land. Those, on the other hand, who were without employment or support would be interned as POWs under the War Measures Act (WMA).

The WMA – executive-enabling legislation introduced to uphold order and protect the peace – permitted unfettered discretion with regard to how this was to be achieved.[12] This led to a broad definition of security, which enabled unemployed enemy aliens to be cast as a security threat while still allowing for them to continue functioning in the economy. The idea of unemployed enemy alien labour as a security threat would become a key characteristic of the Canadian internment experience and would distinguish Canada in the global history of First World War internments.[13]

Critically, the securitization of the enemy alien problem was not without complications. The war convention allowed for the use of POW labour, ostensibly providing a mechanism for managing enemy alien joblessness. Yet the truth of the matter was that these were indigent civilians who happened to be interned. Thus, the contradictory status of simultaneously being both POWs and interned civilians was addressed by drawing on the idea that these people were civilian POWs. This hybrid designation proved useful. Ambiguity in international law accompanied this description, allowing for interpretation and even for the denial of any wrongdoing.[14] Still, Canada's interpretation subjected its claim to criticism, placing the legitimacy of Canadian internment into question.

The assertion that both enemy alien internment and enemy alien labour were lawful had to be justified. The link between political decision making in Canada and the constitutional imperatives of peace, order, and good government gave weight to the view that internment was needed to ensure stability. This conferred the semblance of legitimacy on the decisions taken by senior officials.[15] So, when they argued that internment was introduced as a form of relief – purportedly to safeguard the peace – this reasoning went unchallenged since it conformed to the idea that the decision to intern fell not only within the scope of the government's constitutional powers but also its lawful domestic activity and responsibilities. After all, municipal and provincial governments regularly dealt with the poor. Enemy alien impecuniousness was said to be no different.

This reinterpretation of internment as a domestic affair blurred the distinction between military prisoners and civilian internees. It would have enormous implications, becoming a consequential feature of the Canadian internment experience. On the one hand, the unresolved juridical question of prisoner status bore directly on the way internment would be conducted.[16] On another level, the rights and obligations of prisoners constituted a charged political question in so far as its propaganda value attracted the attention of Germany, making it one of the few diplomatic issues with which Canada contended during the war.[17] But the issue of rights and obligations also called attention to even deeper questions: How could innocent civilians who chose to settle in Canada be treated as war prisoners? And did such individuals even belong?

In the ensuing diplomatic dispute, Canada's manoeuvring became a significant but not well-understood aspect of the internment story – one that underscored not only the indefinite nature of international law at the time but also the connection between the local and the international dimensions of internment. Although frequently treated as a discrete, stand-alone phenomenon, Canadian internment is linked to wider global developments – notably, transnational migration and international conflict. Situating Canada in the world, the impact of globalization is highlighted, connecting what occurred in Canada to the phenomenon of internment as a universal practice.[18] So, too, did Canada's link to Britain, which located Canadian internment within the context of an imperial network with its own logic, preferences, and priorities.[19] Still, the issue remained the same: migrant fit was problematic, especially in a world at war. Once unwanted, and without political checks, the response became a familiar one.

In the end, the ambiguous status of enemy aliens behind barbed wire exposed the impossible nature of Canada's position. Confronted with trying to reconcile the dilemma, the government vacillated in its reasoning and explanations – civilians yet POWS, POWS yet civilians.[20] At the core of government equivocation was scepticism about the place of the enemy alien in Canadian society. For, even though they were a social and political liability, they were still economically necessary.[21] Yet, for the Anglo-majority, there was no mistaking who these people were. Internalizing the civilizational character of the struggle, patriotic lines of demarcation were drawn: "us" versus "them." But how would civilizational concern translate into xenophobia? What was the process that moved public opinion from bias to belligerence, resentment to retribution? And how would the government be moved to act? An issue of significance, but not entirely understood, is this intersection between internment policy and public opinion.

War, of course, is a serious undertaking and the stakes are high. If war is to be successfully prosecuted, a narrative detailing its importance must be carefully crafted and conveyed. Information that is propagated to promote a particular narrative – that is, propaganda – features prominently in this effort.[22] For such a narrative to resonate, however, it must include recognizable elements. Thus, even though the fight was far away, the enemy had to be near. And though the conflict was abstract, it had to be seen as immediate. The danger, in effect, had to be understood as both real and present.[23]

Prewar stereotypes of the migrant contributed to identifying the threat, as did economic uncertainty and the potential for labour unrest.[24] But, on their own, could class or "race" sufficiently drive public antipathy? After all, enemy aliens were part of the larger working class and end-of-century mass migration. These wider constituencies were not subjected to similar levels of umbrage and suspicion. So why target this category of individual?

With empires at war and imperial identity entrenched, who enemy aliens were said to be and what they represented acquired a more complex meaning. Their presence – already manifestly problematic – assumed a more sinister character as identity became increasingly militarized within the context of war.[25] They were the enemy, and the official enemy alien classification, which exposed them to internment as war prisoners, simply reinforced this point of view. War, then, would increasingly frame the public's attitude, attributing all manner of sins to those who did not belong, resulting in rumours, accusations, and allegations.

But if they were the enemy, why were so many of them at liberty? Clearly an issue, how this fact evolved into a policy debate regarding a course of action is less evident. Security measures were in place, but the wider public saw the government response as languid and in need of being strengthened. The press, as self-described guardians of the public interest, assumed a pivotal role, focusing on the conspicuousness of the apparent threat.[26] Still, for the message to be understood, and for the government to be persuaded to act, public opinion had to be channelled. So, whether it was the perceived indolence of the enemy alien, the wholesale conscription of enemy alien labour, or dealing with "enemy" political and labour activists, the press advocated for a more robust government response to protect the country, highlighting these issues as well as others for consideration.[27] Little effort, howerver, was required to convince an anxious public: the problem was already widely seen as exigent.

By mobilizing public opinion in favour of internment, the press pressured the government to act more vigorously. This alignment between the press, public opinion, and the government helps to explain the making and shaping of internment policy.[28] Still, even though, throughout the process, the focus on fit remained the same, for economic reasons the government viewed internment less as a tool to be broadly used and more as an instrument of selective control. This suggested prudence on the government's part and a desire to avoid risk.

For the Anglo-majority there were no such constraints. The attitude towards the enemy alien, especially that of returning veterans, remained conspicuously hostile.[29] Since the enemy had no place in the country, a more forceful internment – seen as a natural extension of the war – was promoted. Between prudence and hostility, however, there was considerable space for interpretation regarding the treatment of those behind barbed wire. What the experience of the camps would reveal was not only the reality of internment but also its deeper meaning – a practice rooted in both suspicion and dislike of the foreigner.

First-hand accounts of what took place in the camps are rare, and the record, therefore, incomplete.[30] Nevertheless, from official archival sources broad strokes can be gleaned. For those in the camps, conditions on the frontier were harsh, work arduous, and the isolation psychologically devastating. To extract labour and enforce obedience the internees were subjected to violence and frequent threats of punishment. Symptomatic of deeper impulses at work, the internees were abused and exploited as a matter of course. The cruel nature of their ordeal commands our attention. And rightly so. Only by recognizing the brutality of the experience can we appreciate what was endured and, consequently, better understand its lessons.

Indeed, the toil and torment were not coincidental. They occurred because the uncertainty in the legal status of the interned enemy alien fuelled opportunity, ambition, and resentment. Although the prisoners proclaimed their innocence, their protests were ignored. Having nothing to do with the war, the internees could not fathom why they were imprisoned let alone forced to labour as POWs. In their bewilderment, however, lay an important byline of the internment story: once imprisoned, they were disavowed because they did not fit. Thus, their plight was seen as inconsequential, requiring neither explanation nor justification, adding to the callous and surreal nature of the experience.[31]

In the end, the origins of the enemy alien experience were ordinary. Rooted in rejection, it mattered less what these people did than who they were said to be. Still, the promise of settlement was that, through a sharing of responsibilities, a home could be created. That the idea of home was embroiled in the politics of belonging ensured it would be a contested issue.[32] Thus, no matter how strong the desire, the promise of settlement remained unfulfilled. Meanwhile, for those in the camps, there was no mistaking their predicament: there was no place for them, and the idea of home was but an illusion.

During the Great War, conflict became the lens through which many experiences of the day were filtered. Internment in Canada is no exception. Considered largely unfortunate, internment nevertheless is interpreted as a natural consequence of war.[33] Its use as a security measure is said to have been legitimate and not callously intended. The difficulty with this argument, however, is that it does not align with the evidence. The evidence points to the selective targeting of destitute and jobless migrants of Austro-Hungarian, German, and Ottoman origin among the wider pool of unemployed in the country, where some 8,579 enemy aliens were interned in twenty-four camps across Canada and more than eighty thousand were required to register as part of an extensive surveillance system. Among the interned, political "undesirables" could be counted, and, at the conclusion of the war, officials sought their removal from the country as well. In the end, what determined their arrest, internment, and registration was not the conflict but their problematic fit within Canadian society, which allowed for them to be watched, imprisoned, and even deported at war's end.

Fit and belonging are recurring themes in the story of First World War Canadian internment. These are at the heart of the following chapters, which, in their detail and analysis, help us to understand more completely those issues and events that gave shape to the internment experience: the enigmatic character of Canadian political identity and the uncertain status of immigrants in Canadian law, which made the alien of enemy origin vulnerable to internment (chapter 1); the circumstances behind the introduction of security legislation that resulted in the internment of civilian migrants of enemy origin as POWs (chapter 2); the rationale behind the blurring of the civilian/military prisoner distinction and its concurrent effect on the practice of internment and war diplomacy (chapter 3); the dynamic between public opinion, the press, and government in British Columbia regarding the purging of enemy aliens from the province and country (chapter 4); and, finally, the experience and character of internment in Banff and Kapuskasing as palpable expressions of enemy alien repudiation and rejection (chapters 5 and 6).

The notion of belonging marks a way to connect the various aspects of the story of internment. It points to the idea that war amplified the problem of fit but did not create it. Thus, security was not the driving force behind internment; rather, it was the consequence of a deeper scepticism about the role and place of migrants in Canada, culminating in the debates at the conclusion of the war about the future of immigration. Still, this was war, and, more especially, it was war between empires that transformed the issue of birthright from problem into threat. Who the immigrants were said to be mattered more than what they did – a sentiment that Canada, relying as it did on immigration, could ill afford.

Because of their centrality to the issue of nationhood, questions of belonging and fit are constant. They are also important because an inherent feature of immigration is the promise of a future – namely, that there will be a home for those who come to Canada. The tragedy experienced by John Kondro and others – embodied in their internment – was the betrayal of that promise. This is not always understood or appreciated in the story of internment. However, by acknowledging their trials and perseverance, we are able not only to grasp what happened and why, but also, more important, to discern its impact on ordinary people. Yet this can only occur if history and its lessons are uncovered, highlighting for us the need for remembrance (Epilogue). Only by accurately recalling what occurred, by placing at the centre of the experience the stories of those who endured, can we be alerted to the shortcomings of leadership and retain lessons regarding how we might deal with present-day challenges – an important feature of redress.[34]

The following chapters are organized around the ideas of fit, belonging, and home. These are themes central to the internment and immigration stories. They speak to longing and need – both fulfilled and unfulfilled. This is especially true of the notion of home, which is both an idea and a reality, a construct located partly in imagination, aspiration, and the materiality of the here and now. This makes for a complicated narrative. But the prospect of desire turning into reality is what makes the allegory of home so powerful. The hope is always that a home awaits us all. When this hope falls short, we still try to achieve it by returning to the promise of the future as both a guide and a compass. To get to this point, however, we must turn to the historical record and remember so that we may understand what went wrong and why. And then, with this understanding, determine what we must do next.

1

The Predicament of Belonging

The Status of Enemy Aliens in Canada, 1914

Before the First World War, mass conscription made acceptable the general proposition that civilians of foreign nationality residing in countries engaged in war might be interned. The result was that the internment of those who originated from enemy lands – including civilians – became a widely adopted practice among the belligerents during the Great War. Importantly, interned enemy alien civilians were not the same as combatants captured on the field of battle and interned. A distinction between the two was made and generally respected among all the belligerents. Indeed, apart from reservists and merchant marines (deemed combatants under international law), it was accepted that interned civilians of enemy nationality were not to be treated as military prisoners of war (POWs). In effect, they were to be spared the rigours associated with military captivity. Remarkably, Canada did not observe this distinction but, rather, treated interned civilian aliens of enemy origin as POWs.

Many of these individuals were placed in wilderness camps under military supervision and subjected to a regime of compulsory labour. The internment of enemy aliens as war prisoners (in some cases until 1920, when a formal peace treaty was concluded) raises important questions about the status of immigrants in

Canada and the broader Canadian political context that existed before the First World War.[1] Given that these individuals were actively recruited to Canada at the turn of the century and invited to settle the land, the question of how a government could so quickly change its position by interning and treating them as captured military combatants is perplexing, to say the least.

The indefinite nature of international law respecting the rights of interned civilians provided the context in which these people would be denied the considerations widely believed owing to non-combatants.[2] This, however, does not entirely explain why Canada chose to treat interned civilian enemy aliens as military POWs. After all, the same lack of clarity in international law did not have a bearing on the treatment of civilian enemy prisoners elsewhere. For example, in the United States, a distinction was generally maintained and conditions in the camps were largely humane.[3] Of far greater importance in explaining the vulnerability of enemy aliens, and of immigrants more generally, was their uncertain place in Canadian law. A consequence of the divided or incomplete nature of Canadian sovereignty and the unresolved puzzle of Canadian political identity, the non-British subject status of immigrants not only made their standing in the community tenuous but also, in the end, both provided for their internment as aliens of enemy origin and allowed for their abject treatment while interned.

Importantly, the problematic status of the alien's place in the community – a question of belonging – paralleled a deeper conflict between two competing paradigms that then dominated Canadian public discourse regarding nationality and political community. Nationalism and imperialism – the two competing paradigms – not only outlined divergent views about political identity but also provided a framework for many of the policy decisions that were made during this period of national challenge and trial. The idea of citizenship, for example, championed by the government of Sir Wilfrid Laurier in the late nineteenth century, flowing out of a liberal nationalist understanding of the polity, had provided a theoretical basis for the political incorporation of the mass of newly arrived immigrants invited to Canada. The model, which maintained that immigrants could be understood as rights-bearing individuals, logically suited a settler polity like Canada. However, because of the extenuating circumstances governing Canadian sovereignty, nationalism could not be fully adopted as the basis for the legal incorporation of immigrants.

Canada's status as a dominion, a residual product of the British imperial legacy, meant that Canada exercised sovereignty only in the domestic arena, while external sovereignty – a matter of continuing political and diplomatic importance to Great Britain – remained very much within the purview of His Majesty's government in London.[4] Accordingly, because Canadian immigration and naturalization law (which determined the legal place of aliens in Canada) fell within the external domain, these laws had to fit within the existing imperial framework. Canada in effect could not adjust its notions of belonging unilaterally but, rather, had to ensure that its legislation was consistent with imperial statutory law, for it was imperial law that expressed the wishes of Canada's external sovereign.

Significantly, the idea of Canada promoted by imperialists was congruent with the imperial legal code in that the legal status of individuals was defined by their relationship, as subjects, to the Crown.[5] With the imperialist Borden government in power from 1911 on, this meant that subjectship was ascendant as both a political and legal idea. Subjectship defined an individual's status by their relationship with the Crown. This suggested not only that individuals received protection and benefits directly from the Crown but also that those with an unclear relationship to the Crown, such as aliens, would receive only limited rights.

In and of itself, this limitation would have been of little importance, but the stress of war required that the government respond to practical problems raised by the presence of so many enemy aliens in Canada, particularly concerns about security and welfare. Retreating from the citizenship conception of the polity – which had facilitated the original settlement of those soon to be reclassified as enemy aliens – and relying on conventional and more expedient notions associated with the imperial view of belonging, the government gradually began to define Canada's success and identity in terms of its imperial contribution to the war. This shift had enormous implications for immigrants of enemy nationality generally. More important, it would have direct bearing on the treatment of those civilian enemy aliens interned as prisoners of war.

Until recently, the doctrine of sovereign right made no provision for individuals in international law. As a result, individuals existed in international law only in so far as their respective government recognized and represented them. Following this understanding, the doctrine of sovereign right assured that decisions governing the status of individuals were the responsibility of the state. Since international law did not interfere with the freedom of sovereign states to determine citizenship independently, no general guidelines existed as to how individuals were to belong. For Canada, a dominion of the British Empire and therefore not a fully sovereign state, this presented a special problem.

Indeed, although Canada had its own naturalization laws, the defining political characteristic of Canadians, at least until 1946, was that they were subjects of the British Crown. This status, defined by common law doctrine, had evolved without significant change from principles invoked in the Calvin case of 1608.[6] It did not mean that a Canadian nationality failed to exist. On the contrary, the imperial structure that divided Canadian sovereignty into its external and internal aspects also made an allowance for a two-tiered nationality. In this regard, Canada created its own category of naturalization – Canadian citizenship. This, however, was merely an administrative convenience. Only British law could make a person a full British subject, and only subject status entitled an individual to belong fully in the Canadian polity. Constrained by an imperial legacy that divided Canadian sovereignty, Canada could not define who fully belonged to the country.

Like Canadian sovereignty, the development of a legally recognized Canadian nationality before the First World War was the result of ad hoc adjustments rather than of a defining legislative act. As with Canadian sovereignty, the crucial distinction was the difference between national and imperial areas of responsibility. This division of responsibility meant that the status of individuals was defined by three sorts of statutes: laws relating to British subject status, Canadian naturalization law, and Canadian immigration law.

The most important of these categories was British subject status, defined by the United Kingdom's 1870 Naturalization Act. It applied to the entire empire, so that someone born in Toronto or Montreal, just like someone born in London, automatically became a British subject. However, the Naturalization Act, 1870, also stated that the only way for an immigrant from outside the empire to acquire British subject status was to reside in the United Kingdom for five years and then take the oath of allegiance there. An immigrant could not become a British subject in a dominion; thus, an immigrant to Canada could not obtain a status that was valid throughout the empire. It was left up to each dominion to decide how immigrants who arrived in its territory without having acquired British subject status could join the polity.

Generally, dominions chose to create a mechanism whereby an immigrant could be naturalized.[7] In Canada, Canadian citizenship was the mechanism created, notably through the Naturalization Act, 1906, which not only allowed the naturalization of immigrants in Canada but, when combined with the 1910 Immigration Act, also defined Canada's immigration policy.[8] The Immigration Act created what one scholar characterizes as an ad hoc distinction between Canadian citizens and others. Only Canadian citizens, not British subjects in general, could enter Canada without being inspected by immigration authorities, a distinction that infamously gave Canadian authorities the legal authority to discriminate against individuals attempting to immigrate to Canada from British possessions in the Orient.[9] The 1910 Immigration Act also created the unusual situation that the only people who were Canadian citizens without being British subjects were immigrants who had met Canada's requirements in the 1881 or 1906 Naturalization Acts but who had not been able to claim British subject status. For those of non-British stock, only being born in Canada would allow them to claim subject status and thus full membership in the Canadian polity.

While the statute law explicitly stated that naturalized and native-born subjects had the same rights, the imperial structure into which these categories fit undermined any attempt at a liberal notion of immigration. Subjects had links to the empire; citizens did not. Subjects, in effect, were full members of the polity because they could relate to the Crown in both its internal (Canadian) and external (British) aspects. Naturalized Canadian citizens, however, could relate only to Canada.[10] Accordingly, in the context of war, the position of the naturalized immigrant was difficult because the immigrant had no attachment to that aspect of the polity that was the most important in wartime. Furthermore, the immigrant's place in and acceptance by society would be determined by norms of loyalty that could be neither easily nor readily satisfied.

The relationship of naturalized Canadian citizens to the Crown was at best tenuous. The fact that their place in Canada could be revoked by the government at any time simply underscored their predicament.[11] In this regard, naturalization failed to grant its holder either full or secure status. Yet, despite this insecurity, naturalized Canadians were still better off than unnaturalized aliens, who, by definition, were completely outside the polity. Having no relationship with the Crown from which they could gain rights and having no contracting relationship with the community in which they resided, the unnaturalized alien – the proverbial stranger – operated not only on the margins of society but also at the mercy and discretion of others, a vulnerability that was made abundantly clear with the onset of war.

The legal notions that centred on sovereignty were rendered even more problematic for enemy aliens because of how imperialists, politically ascendant at the outbreak of war, understood the Canadian national project and the status of subjects. For imperialists, subject status was more than a legal reality; it was also a desirable normative prescription for how individuals ought to belong to the polity. As Carl Berger notes, during the early part of the twentieth century the imperialist perspective, which defined Canada as a member of the British Empire, was much more influential than nationalism.[12] Led by George Grant, Stephen Leacock, George Denison, and others, the imperialist movement in Canada had the support of a significant portion of the population, its strength being derived in part from the imperialists' adroit use of national history, especially their characterization of the United Empire Loyalists and French Canadians as the ideal types of imperial subjects in Canada. According to the imperialists, belonging to Canada meant being loyal to the British Crown.[13] Thus, both French Canadians and United Empire Loyalists were true Canadians because they remained loyal to the Crown during the American wars of 1776 and 1812. For imperialists, it was only through loyalty and sacrifice that full political membership in Canada could be achieved.

Defining the Canadian nation in terms of loyalty to the British Crown, however, created a contradiction in the imperialist position. Despite the importance of Quebec, imperialists saw British cultural and political practices as models for the country.[14] French culture and language in Quebec would be respected because of past loyalty and sacrifices, but outside of Quebec any attempt to build a bilingual or bicultural country was categorically rejected since it would interfere with Canada's imperial mission. The situation of non-British immigrants who had no demonstrable history of loyalty to the Crown meant that they would be assimilated into Anglo-Canadian society.[15] The belief was that it would require much time and effort for a nation to be formed from these people, especially in the case of Eastern Europeans, who, from an imperialist perspective, were thought to be culturally and politically unprepared for life in Canada.

Not only did imperialists hold to a vision of Canada in which the role of non-British immigrants was difficult to ascertain, they also subscribed to a vision of political belonging – subjectship – that made incorporating new members into the polity difficult to achieve. To be sure, by serving the British Crown immigrants could undergo an experience of loyalty and so become full members of Canada, like the United Empire Loyalists and French Canadians. It was, however, an opportunity that would be denied immigrants given their proscribed status as "aliens," whose loyalty, it was concluded, lay elsewhere. Aliens, in short, were outside the polity, without a way to enter it with a full and secure status.

Significantly, the allegiance of the alien was thought to rest elsewhere because of the nature of the relationship between Crown and subject. First, this relationship has its origins in the state of nature: before the polity is formed, individuals are linked to a strongman, a king.[16] Allegiance to a Crown exists prior to any other allegiance because it is a natural link determined by God. As a result of this reasoning, English law long affirmed that no subject could replace one sovereign with another; an individual, by becoming a subject of another Crown, simply acquired a second loyalty. Should the two Crowns engage in war, British law expected that primary allegiance would be given to the Crown under which the individual had been born.[17]

Second, subject status envisioned a polity based on hierarchy. In the state of nature, hierarchy had already been established when individuals gave up their autonomy to a king. When the polity was formed, there was no reason to alter that hierarchy. Different individuals could be accorded a different status without affecting the basic notion of the polity.[18] Because immigrants were newcomers to a polity that was based on loyalty, they could be granted a lesser status without disrupting the definition of the polity. Finally, subjects owed allegiance and loyalty to the king, and the king, in return, extended protection to the subject.[19] Subjectship, in effect, was viewed as a relationship based on dominance and subordinance in which the subject's duty was to be passively loyal. It was a relationship in which legal protection was extended in return for loyalty (yet to be demonstrated, in the case of immigrants) rather than as an inherent right.

For aliens of enemy origin, the imperialist understanding of political subject status meant two things. On one level, it allowed the government to view them as a possible security threat.[20] This seemed a fair expectation since, by virtue of the political obligation that was framed by the idea of subjectship, they would serve the Crown under which they had been born.[21] On another level, it conditioned their treatment. Membership in the polity entailed loyalty, and loyalty was proven through service. The military underpinnings of subjectship became self-evident: civilians of enemy nationality could be treated as members of an opposing military whether or not they were directly engaged in the conflict. The implications for internment were plain. As subjects of a sovereign at war with the British Empire, they could be considered, given this expanded view, not simply as interned civilians but war prisoners to which the practices if not the laws of war would apply.[22]

While subjectship defined the legal status of immigrants and represented one vision of their place in the Canadian project (a vision that proved dominant in wartime) there was yet another perspective regarding the place of immigrants in Canada – that of citizenship. Although marginalized during the war years, a citizenship-based understanding of Canada remained important because, under the Laurier government, it tentatively framed the political place of immigrants in the country.[23] Citizenship, the nationalists argued, was the only mechanism by which immigrants might be incorporated into the body politic. Moreover, by conceiving of such individuals as potential citizens, the possibility was created that they might eventually contribute to the polity as equals. More specifically, the development of the Canadian west through agricultural settlement would facilitate their entry into the community as full participants, ensuring their place in the evolving community.[24]

The idea of citizenship in the Anglo-American tradition had a twofold importance. First, it took from Lockean conceptions of the state of nature the idea that autonomous individuals gathered and contracted to form a polity, therefore entering the polity as equals and of their own free will. Since the polity's founding experience is contractual, the citizenship model argues that a newcomer joins the polity on the same basis as the native-born and that an individual's decision to accede to that contract is the same whenever it takes place. If individuals agree to join a polity, they are, in effect, accepted on terms like those that govern the founding members, with no history of loyalty necessary to become a full member of the polity. The model of citizenship, furthermore, suggests that the relationship between government and individual changes once a government is established. Instead of passive loyalty, citizens are encouraged to participate actively in government, while imposed service is shunned since service without choice does little to help individuals learn what membership in the polity means and what obligations it entails. From the perspective of citizenship, aliens are part of the body politic, and the label "enemy" does not apply unless an act of treason is committed.

In the prewar period, the Laurier government actively encouraged large-scale immigration and was the first government that systematically tried to find a place for non-British immigrants in Canada. Recruiting immigrants to help in the economic development of the country meant that, once immigrants arrived, they were encouraged to stay.[25] The intention of government policy, therefore, was to facilitate successful settlement as much as possible. The vital role played by the Canadian state in settlement indicated an instrumental approach to immigration whereby settlement was an activity carried out under government direction in pursuit of a goal beneficial to the overall nation-building project. This approach prescribed a role for the immigrant as potential citizen.

The national project, as it was being realized by the Laurier government, was a compromise between the desire to make the country grow and the desire to cultivate a new civic identity within the context of the still dominant imperial political and cultural framework.[26] The nurturing of this complicated nationality was largely the responsibility of the Canadian state, testing policymakers who struggled to reconcile the contradictory nature of the need for immigration with the political and legal implications of the imperialist perspective. The nationalists attempted to deal with the complexity of Canada by building a civic nation. Their perspective on Canadian nationality achieved real results in encouraging hundreds of thousands of immigrants to come to Canada. They did not, however, succeed either in creating a definite legal category for immigrants or in conceptualizing the place of immigrants in the country. Nor did they articulate how they might belong in such a way that their loyalty could be guaranteed to the satisfaction of imperialist feeling or reconciled with the sentiments embedded in the imperial legal code.

With the onset of the First World War, nascent notions of a civic nation were displaced by the still robust imperialist perspective, one that not only more clearly defined state and society but that was also congruent with imperial law. The lucidity of the imperial perspective made the making of policy pertaining to aliens easier for the government. It also, however, presented an oversimplified vision of Canada that would have immense implications for the tens of thousands of enemy aliens in the country.

Despite support from nationalists and a pragmatic need to increase immigration, prewar immigration policy failed to overcome the constraints imposed on Canada by its incomplete sovereignty and the associated problem of subject status. The outbreak of the First World War saw a retreat from nationalist notions of political incorporation based on citizenship to the traditional concepts of empire and subject status. This retreat would eventually place aliens of enemy origin in a tenuous position because a more definitive political relationship between immigrants and the Canadian polity had not yet been established.

The retreat to an imperialist understanding of Canada during the war took two forms. First, while the liberal nationalist perspective had attempted to accommodate immigrants as potential citizens, imperialism and imperial legal structures dictated not only that non-British immigrants of enemy birthright were prohibited from being fully incorporated within the polity but they were also deemed enemies. Enemy aliens were vulnerable because they were considered "outside" the Canadian polity and, as subjects of a foreign power with which Canada was at war, their allegiance was determined to lie elsewhere. Moreover, the treatment of foreign subjects of enemy nationality as enemy combatants followed logically and naturally from an imperial sentiment that made clear distinctions about allegiance, loyalty, and service.

Second, the retreat towards an imperialist conception of Canada changed the nature of the Canadian nation-building project. Prior to the war, the emphasis had been on western settlement, which created a clear need for immigrants and defined a way for settlers to contribute to and thus participate in the political formation of Canada. War, however, refocused the national project from the wheatfields of western Canada to the battlefields of Flanders. As subjects of an enemy Crown, enemy aliens could not be trusted to serve in an imperial army.[27] From this perspective, not only did they seemingly have little to contribute to the political project that was Canada but also it was no longer necessary to find a political place for them. Building a life in a new country – a task that was suffused with political meaning in the latter half of the nineteenth century – was, in 1914, of incidental value and had little political merit.

Given the magnitude of these changes, it is unsurprising that the retreat to an imperial framework took shape slowly. In August 1914, with the war's start, a certain amount of effort was made to retain the prewar nationalist conception that non-British immigrants, including aliens born in enemy lands, were members of Canadian society. The Royal Proclamation of 15 August 1914, for example, made a distinction between "our subjects" and "all persons resident," and stated that aiding or abetting the enemy would lead to the charge of treason. Treason implied that certain offences were deemed acts against a community of which one was part.[28] Similarly, the Royal Proclamation specified security measures aimed at controlling enemy aliens but offered the assurance that aliens of enemy birthright would not be interfered with if they pursued their ordinary avocations peacefully.[29] The implication, again, was that there was a place for those who abided by society's rules.

This assurance was repeated in a public notice issued 2 September 1914, when the government, learning of the fear among immigrants of enemy origin that "some Government action might deprive them of their freedom," declared that apprehension among this segment of the population was unfounded.[30] The public notice was meant to allay the anxiety of those who feared that they were not part of the community or thought that they faced the threat of being treated as such. These assurances were meant to go beyond a simple acknowledgment of coexistence. The assurances signalled a general obligation on the part of the government, while also acknowledging commitment on the part of the settlers who laboured for their own benefit and that of the country.

The opening weeks and months of the war, however, saw two major developments that would affect government policy towards aliens of enemy nationality. Foremost, there was a hardening of public and elite attitudes towards enemy aliens as foreign subjects. This attitude, in the context of heightened insecurity, forced the government to adopt an increasingly ambivalent position regarding enemy aliens. As thousands of aliens migrated to the international border – hoping to cross in search of work and refuge – hundreds were arrested by border officials who, suspecting the worst, dutifully acted on government instructions prohibiting the departure of enemy aliens. The government also issued successive orders-in-council to bolster the capacity of local authorities to safeguard installations while reducing the risk of an imagined threat. This activity added to the excited state of a population already primed by wild rumours of sabotage and idle talk of espionage. The combination of the government's retreat to a more defensive posture on domestic security and the public's perception about perceived threats underscored not only the existing "outsider" status of enemy aliens within Canadian society but also their diminished social and political role in the national life of the country. This set a course of action that would make further policy measures appear, if not necessary, then at least logical and appropriate.

The level of unemployment and poverty among the ethnic immigrant underclass was no less important and was also a contributing factor. Throughout September and early October of 1914, policy-makers took an ad hoc approach to finding solutions to the growing unemployment problem among this group. Nevertheless, their numbers continued to swell. Being responsible for the unemployed, cities and towns were unable to cope with the subsequent destitution of this mass of people. Ottawa had to be involved. To be sure, the economic recession led to thousands from all backgrounds being put out of work. However, it was the enemy alien – the outsider whose place in society was uncertain and status as a foreign subject unclear – who would bear the burden of a faltering economy. Managers, owners, and even unions decided that enemy aliens should be the first to be dismissed from places of work. The increased need for poor relief, then, was paired with a strongly felt need to define the status of the enemy alien.

Across the country, the story was much the same as countless numbers of enemy aliens began to migrate between cities and towns in search of work and relief. From the government's perspective, the prospect of thousands of enemy subjects roaming about among a public galvanized by spirited talk of empire and conflict was unsettling, necessarily raising important questions about what, if any, obligation Canada had to this class of individual. Several cabinet members felt a need to provide for the material well-being of aliens. In the context of war, however, where loyalty to the Crown was at a premium and society was being exhorted to serve in its defence, any discussion about the obligation owed to settlers of enemy birthright was cut short, complicating the hard and fast, yet useful, distinctions that were being shaped by the struggle at hand. The eventual response to this growing crisis – the War Measures Act and the widespread internment of enemy aliens – corresponded closely to imperial notions of belonging and loyalty, dealing cleanly, if harshly, with issues of obligation. Placing enemy aliens, now labelled POWs, in primitive internment camps far away from public view reinforced the idea that nothing was owed these people.

In the end, the Canadian government's response to the difficulty posed by the enemy alien was less the result of an incomplete understanding of the situation on the ground than a failed conceptualization regarding belonging and the polity. The First World War, with its demands on Canada, made imperialism a generally more appealing way to understand the country than nationalism because the former could solve the difficult issues of belonging and loyalty in a time of national crisis. There were definite limitations to this model – notably, preventing settler-immigrants, especially those of enemy origin, from belonging to the Canadian polity. The failure of this model was made apparent in the consequences of the policies that alienated significant numbers of individuals who had to negotiate a place in Canadian society after the war. It was also unsustainable given that Canada, dependent on immigration, would become a citizenship-based polity one day.

2

Security and the Outsider

Managing the Enemy Alien Problem in Canada, 1914

In Canada at the outset of the Great War, thousands of immigrants originating from states warring with Britain and the empire, so-called enemy aliens, were arrested and interned as POWs. Tens of thousands more registered with local authorities and reported regularly under an extensive monitoring regime. As foreign subjects liable to mobilization, aliens of enemy origin were considered potential recruits for opposing armies. Therefore, the security measures adopted fell well within the legal purview of the Canadian state to defend itself. It is from this broad perspective that the question of how internment came to pass in Canada is explained. Still, in an age of large-scale migration, world war, and mass mobilization, security entailed new complexities. A deft if not nuanced response was required. So how, then, was security defined with respect to the alien of enemy origin and how did security interests inform government policy, decisions, and actions taken towards this class of people? What conditions – economic, social, political – dictated the use of war measures? And did these conditions meet the bar of necessity, or were they simply sufficient to declare an emergency without considering its possible effects?

A state of emergency declaration is a high-risk venture with manifold consequences. In the pursuit of security, the tension that exists between vigilance and caution should normally have led to careful deliberation regarding the implementation of security measures.[1] Yet in the early months of the war there was little substantive discussion about the implications of specific decrees – the 15 August 1914 Royal Proclamation and the 28 October 1914 Order-in-Council PC 2721 issued under the War Measures Act – that made internment a likely outcome for the enemy alien. The edicts, with their force of law, appeared to contradict the normative understanding, which holds that security measures are to be used sparingly and carefully. So, what did the government's actions disclose about its intentions?

Creating the conditions for stability and security, laws look to ensure that order is maintained and justice served. By introducing guidelines and parameters, the Royal Proclamation and Order-in-Council PC 2721 sought to manage the enemy alien problem. Arguably, order was achieved in the process. Yet what of justice? What responsibility did the government have to these people as settlers, or put differently, what, if any, ethical considerations factored into the strategic calculus that led to decisions that so greatly affected the unsuspecting and innocent?

At first glance, security and justice appear to be at cross-purposes. However, the issues and questions associated with each, weighty in their import, suggest that justice and security are not incompatible if immigrants are recognized as being within the Canadian polity. The decrees, in this sense, highlight the problem of acceptance. But why was there a problem if they had been invited to the country? The explanation can be found in the logic and rationale behind the use of the edicts and the unfolding story that was internment.

As the clouds of war gathered over Europe, reservists in Canada were called home to serve in the armies of their countries of origin. In deference to authority and coupled with concern for their families, hundreds of men of various nationalities, including Germans and those from the Austro-Hungarian Empire, departed for home. Once war was declared, however, the Canadian government saw an urgent need to stem the further return of any remaining reservists. Under the authority of the governor-in-council, a Royal Proclamation was issued on 15 August that made it plain that reserve enemy officers or soldiers would be arrested and detained if they attempted to leave the country. Although the declaration identified a specific category of individual – the reservist – the restriction on leaving Canada necessarily applied to virtually every able-bodied male of enemy origin since, in an age of mass mobilization, all were potential combatants.

The prohibition on departure was an important early security step, an acknowledgment of the fact that Canada was at war. So, too, was another measure outlined in the declaration. Those engaged and suspected of participating in espionage and other hostile acts, or who attempted to aid the enemy, would be apprehended and interned. Enacted on 22 August, the WMA, which delegated extensive emergency powers to the executive, helped facilitate this. Underscoring the concern with security, the WMA demonstrated that little would be left to chance.

The sweeping security powers authorized under the WMA were depicted as vital to the defence of Canada. Still, the government made clear that any measures adopted would be limited. The intent was to secure the realm – no more, no less. In this regard, assurances in the form of a public notice (2 September 1914) were given, indicating that no action would be taken against those who were law-abiding. On this score, the government was unambiguous in its declaration, maintaining that aliens of enemy nationality quietly engaged in their routine pursuits would be allowed to do so without interruption. Furthermore, a provision was included in the Royal Proclamation stating that persons who were arrested and detained would be released if, through a signed undertaking, they pledged not only to abide by the laws of the land and refrain from taking up arms against Canada but also to report regularly to authorities.[2]

While the aim may have been to retain a degree of normality, the Royal Proclamation pre-empted this possibility by impugning the loyalty of aliens of German and Austro-Hungarian extraction. Birthplace was made synonymous with enemy status, and enemy sympathies were presumed because of origin. Although assurances were given that they would not be interfered with if they remained law-abiding, the Royal Proclamation placed in question the loyalty of aliens of enemy origin by suggesting that their natural allegiance was to a foreign sovereign. Because this made them suspect, their relationship with the nation was problematized.[3]

For enemy aliens, the tenuous relationship brought about by their status as foreign subjects created a vulnerability that necessarily shaped public attitudes and government policy. Amidst the economic crisis that gripped Canada at the start of the war and concomitant unemployment within the group, the optics of assisting individuals with presumed foreign allegiances took on significance. Aiding aliens of enemy origin would have undercut the meaning and security intent of the Royal Proclamation. It would also have conveyed the wrong message. Yet the government could not just stand idly by. Given the "outsider" status of the enemy alien in Canadian society, and given the worsening economic conditions, something had to be done. Prohibited from leaving the country to look for work in the United States (as they routinely had done in the past), aliens of enemy origins were now effectively detained.

Their predicament did not go unnoticed. Within a few months of the declaration of war, dispatches to Washington from the US consul general in Montreal, W.H. Bradley, confirmed that the situation facing the enemy alien was grim. A newly appointed neutral diplomat representing Austro-Hungarian interests, Bradley was authorized to assist where he could and report back on what he saw. Within weeks he communicated that, in Montreal alone, four thousand aliens of Austro-Hungarian origin – ethnic Ukrainians, Poles, Croats, and others – had registered for assistance with the diplomatic mission, including two hundred children. Noting their suffering, he observed: "They do not seem evil-disposed, but cannot see why, after being brought here to work, they should be reduced almost to starvation for a war in which they are, apparently, not greatly interested."[4] Although steps had been taken to address the security of the country in the form of the Royal Proclamation, Bradley observed that nothing was being done to alleviate their plight, which, as a result, had appreciably worsened. He felt a national policy was needed to create jobs, especially since the government made of them "virtual prisoners of the country."[5] Moreover, Bradley was perplexed by what appeared to be government indifference since these people were still members of the community – or so he thought.

From Sydney, Nova Scotia, the Reverend M.C. Kinsale corresponded with Secretary of State Thomas Mulvey regarding the serious situation at the local steel works. With mills working at reduced capacity, the owners instituted mass layoffs, mostly affecting Ukrainians and other Eastern Europeans of Austro-Hungarian origin. Noting that it was the Royal Proclamation that prohibited enemy aliens from departing for the US, Kinsale urged that they be allowed to leave as they were in desperate need. He observed through his mission work that these people were not much interested in the war; rather, they were simply in search of employment. Kinsale implored the government to reverse its position on denying exeats since this did nothing to improve security and, in fact, only complicated it. He pleaded with the secretary of state to do right by these men and their families, encouraging the government to let them go. "Take this matter into consideration and find some way out of this difficulty, which, while guaranteeing the safety of the country, will help these men," he beseeched.[6]

The secretary of state wrote to the chief commissioner of the Dominion Police, A.P. Sherwood, asking whether something might be done to meet the needs of the enemy aliens in Sydney. In so doing, the secretary hoped to involve the police. Concerned that he might be drawn into an awkward situation, Sherwood was adamant about the locus of responsibility. He replied that Kinsale's assessment of the state of affairs was correct, adding, however, that the issue had to be resolved politically.[7] The government had sole responsibility for and lone authority to deal with the problem. For Sherwood, the only real question was on what grounds would political decisions be made?

In the absence of government policy and assistance, it was left to the hungry and desperate to do what they could to save themselves. Increasingly, enemy aliens felt compelled to take a chance in crossing the border illegally. Not all succeeded. Mike Kitt was arrested at North Portal, Saskatchewan, for stealing a ride on a freight train to look for work in the Dakotas. Brought before a justice, Kitt explained that, without work and facing starvation, he had no choice but to try to make his way to the US.[8] John Spodarulek was similarly arrested at Brockville, Ontario, attempting to steal across the international line. He confessed to trying to reach the US only because there was no work in Ottawa.[9] Meanwhile, Torn Larivitch and Steve Vincovic could not offer a satisfactory explanation as to why they were on the Grand Trunk train heading from Toronto for the border, although they did inform the arresting officer that there was no work to be had in Brantford, Ontario, where they lived.[10] These handful of cases bore witness to the exodus of individuals who were in grave need, their flight giving testimony to the belief that they could expect little help. Feeling abandoned, they were on their own.

Hardship was experienced across a wide swath of the entire working population of Canada. For enemy aliens, however, the economic situation was especially dire. With the economy continuing to contract and employers facing the choice between hiring those who were native-born and those who were enemy aliens, the latter bore the brunt of unemployment.[11] Preferential hiring, of course, had always been part of normal labour conditions in the country, but with war it assumed a more malign character. The employment practices of businesses and governments alike were increasingly scrutinized by zealots who insisted that loyal British subjects be favoured since, under wartime conditions, birthplace mattered.

In Montreal, a group of English-speaking French and Italian waiters complained to the major local hoteliers that over four hundred individuals of German and Austro-Hungarian origin held remunerative jobs that could just as easily have been occupied by men currently unemployed and "belonging to the Allies."[12] In Calgary, the city commissioner, bowing to public pressure, gave instructions that single men of enemy-alien origin working in the city's street-cleaning department were to be replaced by Britishers since "it would be monstrous to employ members of a nation at war with the British Empire while men of the British race were unable to find employment."[13] In Ottawa, the *Evening Journal* cynically reported that enemy aliens were being favoured with work at the expense of the native-born.[14]

In this heated political climate, businesses were called upon to demonstrate their patriotism and commitment to the empire by hiring only those whose loyalty could be trusted.[15] How could it be otherwise? The 15 August Royal Proclamation already pointed to the unreliability of the enemy subject in the context of war. From the perspective of the patriot, it followed, then, that they be treated as enemies, pointing to an awful yet recurring truth – namely, that wars draw sharp lines between peoples. Notwithstanding the suffering and misery, providing for one's own took precedence over the enemy alien whose intentions and loyalties, a function of birthplace, were suspect.

Still, the task of aiding enemy aliens and their families could not be ignored. Municipal authorities in Ottawa, already distributing hundreds of loaves of bread daily, became increasingly alarmed about the impact that hunger would have on enemy aliens in the city. With want and desperation rampant, the local police feared that riots would soon break out. It was a concern voiced in other parts of the country as well. After the cost of basic foodstuffs increased in Vancouver, unrest was fully expected. When this failed to occur, there was genuine surprise and relief.[16] Meanwhile, in Montreal, the Board of Control was particularly concerned about the possibility of disturbances, recommending to the city council that "it was advisable to send a delegation to Ottawa to confer with the Dominion authorities on the need for additional protection to property in Montreal on account of the foreign element here."[17] City councillors supported the proposal because of a growing belief that the city's enemy alien population posed a threat.

The Charity Organization Society of Montreal estimated that there were five to eight thousand enemy aliens, nearly all of whom were in absolute want, out of work, without funds, and prevented from leaving the country. In the opinion of the charity, they constituted "a serious menace" to the city, one that would grow as the winter approached.[18] Entrusted with public safety, Montreal's chief of police, Oliver Campeau, reported to the city's Board of Control that his officers were helpless to deal with the situation. Campeau observed: "Many hundreds of Austrians and Germans have been thrown out of employment because of their nationality." He added that "robberies and outrages [were] sure to become daily occurrences" and that the police service had few men and even less power to conduct house-to-house searches in the "foreign sections of the city."[19] At a public hearing held to address the issue, those gathered emphatically declared that neither civic authorities nor charitable organizations were equipped to deal with the size and scope of the problem. They called upon the dominion government – "by whose act these men ... are prevented from leaving the country" – to take immediate action.[20]

The government was called to task by a public that had been spurred on by demagogic newspapers, believing that, by failing to take additional steps, officials were doing nothing except making the situation worse. Questions around expectations, indecision, and inaction accounted for the public's displeasure. This criticism, however, ignored the policy goals of the Royal Proclamation and the WMA, which was to augment the security of the country by containing the problem allegedly posed by enemy aliens. The government effectively addressed these goals by initially identifying and isolating enemy aliens as a group while introducing preventative measures to minimize potential threats. It expected the rest to be taken care of through diligent policing. Caution, then, was the watchword. But there were additional reasons to act prudently. The government recognized the potential for unintended consequences. Public anger could quickly escalate, with riots occurring throughout the country. Then there was the unknown effect of targeting the entire enemy alien population, whose continuing participation in the economy, such as it was, remained important. Still, there was no harm in planning – a matter that engaged officials from the start of the war.

As early as August 1914, the minister of defence and militia, Sam Hughes, had identified the need for a policy that more broadly meshed with the country's security needs. Acknowledging that the source of the problem was the prohibition blocking the exit of enemy aliens from the country, the minister stated that, unless the injunction preventing their departure were to be lifted, some scheme had to be devised "for their control and maintenance."[21] The question of control was also on the mind of the industrialist Sir Thomas Shaughnessy of Montreal – a prominent public figure and close confidant of Prime Minister Robert Borden – who, that August, shared his concern over the looming enemy alien situation in the western provinces. From Shaughnessy's perspective: "if these men be permitted to reach a starving condition, they will be dangerous, and, beyond doubt, some steps should be taken to deal with the problem."[22] Shaughnessy proposed the creation of internment camps. His influence, along with the encouragement of Hughes, prompted the prime minister to direct the Department of Militia and Defence, the comptroller of the Royal North-West Mounted Police (RNWMP), and senior ministers to bring forward to cabinet for deliberation and decision a recommendation "that was in the public interest."[23]

Arthur Meighen, solicitor general of Canada, quickly voiced his opposition to the idea of interning jobless enemy aliens. Meighen recommended an alternative – namely, to get them on the land by setting aside parcel lots procured with modest government assistance. "These Austrians," Meighen argued, "are workers as a rule and those I know would jump at the chance to acquire a small piece of land. They can live on very little." Insisting that his plan be given serious consideration, he added, "I realize that there are big difficulties in the way, [but] the necessities are great and the goal is the correct one."[24] When the RNWMP comptroller, Laurence Fortescue, argued that unemployed immigrants of enemy origin be interned in work camps, Meighen reiterated his position that, "by an extension of the homestead system under close Government supervision, a great many of these immigrants [could] be better taken care of."[25] For Meighen, internment was a mistake.

At the senior level of government, opinion was divided on what approach to take. The consequence of disagreement was continuing delay. Yet, with the approaching winter, public impatience and concern over the prospect of an escalation in the crisis made a decision necessary. There was a growing realization that the security question was no longer an abstract exercise the responsibility for which could be offloaded to other levels of government. Ottawa's prohibition on enemy alien departure had exacerbated the problem. More decisive steps were needed.

In late October, worrying about the severity of the unemployment situation with some fifty to one hundred thousand enemy aliens soon expected to be without work, Prime Minister Borden noted: "We must either let them go, provide them with work or feed them; otherwise, they will become desperate and resort to crime."[26] His inclination was to relax the prohibition that prevented enemy aliens from entering the neutral US, especially since there was little probability they would ever reach their homelands. Potentially, however, this had strategic implications for the war, and the prime minister, cognizant of Canada's role in the imperial alliance, wished to solicit and receive as quickly as possible the views and advice of London.

In discussing the matter with the Foreign Office secretary, Canada's high commissioner, Sir George Perley, impressed upon the former that this was a serious question in Canada, largely because of the underlying ethical conundrum: the government had invited these people as immigrants to Canada, and so there was an obligation, according to Perley, to treat the matter with sensitivity.[27] Perley's concerns, however, did not appear to register with British officials. Ignoring the moral dimension and focusing on the practical aspects of the issue, the British foreign secretary, in consultation with the UK colonial secretary, concluded that, despite the expense involved in keeping such a large number under the government's charge – "a serious burden" – the better course of action for the Canadian government was to intern them. Citing the rationale behind the decision, the foreign secretary remarked: "This course, in spite of the expense which it will involve, will no doubt prove the most satisfactory and it will preclude the practical certainty of any Germans or Austrians drifting, by way of the United States of America, back to the enemy's firing line."[28]

The reply from London was clear. Canada had to prevent enemy aliens from joining the fight overseas. Since, through its Royal Proclamation, Canada had already made this class of people out to be enemies, the dire circumstances – to which the government had contributed – could be addressed by using security measures, thus preventing their departure. To this end, and despite the complications, the Canadian government began to take what were now perceived to be further necessary steps.

As pressure mounted on the government to deal with the enemy-alien unemployed, officials were routinely queried about the government's plans. The director of the Philanthropic Society of Montreal, a relief agency that increasingly focused its work on the enemy alien, asked, for example, whether the internment of enemy aliens as POWs was being contemplated as part of the government's strategy.[29] The proposition that these people might be interned as war prisoners, although startling, was not hard to understand. Indeed, in the public mind, the 15 August Royal Proclamation fuelled the notion that aliens with supposed allegiances to an enemy sovereign were foes, contributing to rumours of alleged espionage and treachery. Moreover, once enacted, the sweeping and open-ended nature of the WMA allowed for the widest possible interpretation among the public as to what constituted a threat. Hence, unemployed enemy aliens, seen as a source of potential disturbances, fell within the range of perceived threats. This helped to make publicly acceptable the idea of subjecting them to war measures, including internment as war prisoners.

To be sure, the internment of enemy aliens as POWs was not the aim of the security decrees. On several occasions, the government was unambiguous in its assurances that: "no arrests shall be made unless the persons in question evince an intention of leaving the country for the purpose of fighting against the British Empire, or otherwise assisting the nations with which we are, unfortunately, at war."[30] In addition, under the terms of the 15 August Royal Proclamation, release was all but assured for those who were prepared to sign an undertaking declaring that they would do no harm. In the initial weeks of the war, thousands who had been arrested, either for violation of the regulations or on suspicion, were in fact released. Moreover, in certain quarters, the difficult economic situation confronting the enemy alien elicited sympathy towards them and, hence, apprehension about the steps being proposed. The superintendent of immigration, W.D. Scott, for one, on learning of the desperate plight of enemy aliens in Vancouver, spoke against the idea of interning them: "If the only objection to these people is that they are destitute and unable to provide for themselves, I can scarcely see why they should be refused the same treatment as other immigrants would receive under similar circumstances … I cannot see why they should be treated as military prisoners unless they have done something to bring them within the terms of Clause 2 of the Proclamation of the 15th ultimo."[31]

Officials, nevertheless, had to be mindful of the wider context. This included the government's initial charge identifying these people as individuals not to be trusted, the restriction on enemy aliens leaving the country, and growing unemployment. With pressure mounting, a choice was made. At the prime minister's direction, on 28 October 1914, Charles J. Doherty, minister of justice, submitted a report to cabinet recommending the steps to be taken to further manage the enemy alien problem. That same day the recommendations were adopted and approved by the governor-in-council under the authority of the WMA as Order-in-Council PC 2721.

Derived from the WMA's wide defence and security powers, Order-in-Council PC 2721 was an extraordinary measure. Clause 1 of the ordinance called for the establishment of registration offices in cities and towns where large numbers of enemy aliens were clustered. Appointed registrars were to operate under the supervision of the Dominion Police (Clause 2). Examined and registered, the particulars that would assist in the process of regulating enemy aliens were to be recorded by registrars (Clause 3). Clause 4 required that all enemy aliens within a twenty-mile radius of designated cities and towns register. Clause 5 prohibited aliens of enemy nationality from leaving the country without an exeat granted by a registrar. Clause 7 directed enemy aliens to declare whether they would abide by the laws and customs of the land and had sufficient means to support themselves. On failing to declare in the affirmative or report to police as required, they would be interned as prisoners of war. Clause 7 further stated: "Any alien of enemy nationality who in the judgment of the registrar cannot consistently with the public safety be at large shall be interned as a prisoner of war." Clause 10 authorized the Canadian militia to oversee the maintenance of enemy aliens as prisoners of war, requiring them to do and perform work as deemed fit.

Other orders soon followed under the WMA. Order-in-Council PC 2758, approved on 30 October, identified cities across the country where registration offices would be established: Sydney, Montreal, Ottawa, Fort William, Welland, Winnipeg, Regina, Calgary, and Edmonton (Victoria and Brandon were added after local calls for registration centres there proved effective). Order-in-Council PC 2817, approved on 6 November, designated Major General William Otter as the officer commanding the Internment Operations Directorate. The directorate was placed under the authority of the Department of Justice, although internment was conducted as a military operation since enemy aliens would be interned as POWs. Other executive orders relating to registration and internment were to be introduced as needed. In the main, however, it was PC 2721 that would shape conditions and had the most effect on the greatest number of enemy aliens.

The public announcement accompanying PC 2721 that appeared in the press stated the objective was to effectively control and supervise persons of alien enemy origin.[32] Although acknowledging the majority were perfectly peaceable and posed no threat, the government noted that, potentially, there were enemy aliens who had hostile intentions and, therefore, authorities had an obligation to investigate. Thus, the registration of enemy aliens and, eventually, the internment of those who, in the interest of the public safety, could not be at liberty was seen as both a necessity and a duty. Despite being ambitious in their reach, registration and internment were considered legitimate security measures in the context of war.

Almost as an afterthought the announcement added that those enemy aliens who were not able to maintain themselves would be treated as POWs in accordance with the laws of war, particularly those enacted by the Hague Convention and identified in the convention's Annex. The meaning of the first objective – to intern as war prisoners those who could not safely be at liberty – was now extended to include those who could not provide for themselves. The executive order, in effect, collapsed two categories of individuals. But far more tellingly, in treating both identically, so that those in either category could be interned as POWs, the government gave credence to the idea that the jobless enemy alien posed a security threat. Even so, PC 2721 was not meant to be a blanket order. The impression given was that it was limited and purposeful, and therefore not all that onerous.

Geared towards dealing with those enemy aliens who were without means, the ordinance was taken by some as a good-faith gesture whose purpose was to ease the plight of the enemy alien. Several press reports relayed, for example, that those interned would be provided with "employment opportunities," conveying the idea that internment was a make-work program. Additionally, internment camps were described as places where enemy aliens would be fed and sheltered, suggesting once again that the government was motivated by altruism and fairness. The *Montreal Gazette* argued: "To them a country owes a duty. They came here, some on the invitation of the Government, extended through the immigration service, and some at the suggestion of men who needed their labour. They are generally industrious and would not be idle if they had their choice. They cannot get work, and they cannot return to their homes. Their detention under honorable restriction is the only apparent way of saving most of them from risk of starvation and temptation to crime."[33]

This sense of obligation intimated that there were responsibilities that had to be met. This followed from the relationship of reciprocity that existed between migrants and host country. Immigrants were to play a productive role in the country and, in return, could expect fair treatment. Through no fault of their own, this balance had been interrupted. Now, however, as some believed, it could be nominally restored through internment – a process that could simultaneously address both the joblessness and the welfare of the enemy alien. Without a hint of irony, internment was presented not only as being harmless but also of benefit.

PC 2721 incorporated this inherent dualism. Although the government sought to convey that its intent was not to penalize or harm, the order sanctioned internment as a military operation under which interned enemy aliens, as POWs, were expected to engage in hard, manual labour. How this could be conceived of as harmless or as beneficial stretched credulity. Still, the ordinance was enacted to ensure that the distress of the unemployed enemy alien would not translate into riots and other forms of social unrest. As such, PC 2721 was infused with a particular meaning, perhaps not entirely intended but nonetheless consequential.

The government's approach to the enemy alien was guarded in that it wanted to assist – but within limits. These people, after all, were immigrants of enemy birth, and security had to be maintained. This meant that the process of overseeing them had to be properly managed. In this respect, police and registrars were instructed to exercise diligence regarding the registration of the enemy alien. Supervision and control were to be taken seriously. Thus, registrars were to interrogate enemy aliens brought before them. Answers were to be carefully recorded and copied onto a pass card, which was always to be carried by the registered alien and shown on demand to police, militia, or any other supervising officer. Police were to pay particular attention to the accuracy of the identity documents. Both registrars and police were directed to use judgment in their assessment of personal circumstances, but they were also to be wary of the intentions and attitudes of the enemy alien and communicate: "[any information] which your enquiries may elicit and which you may think advisable to be considered in the public interest."[34] The open-ended nature of the instruction meant that, despite the assurances of non-interference, any reason to intern might suffice.

The wide powers of arrest granted the police and militia, along with the discretionary power of the registrars, became important features of the internment experience. Registration and reporting amounted to a surveillance operation behind which lay the idea that enemy aliens represented a special type of risk. With new powers in hand, the personal views of the police increasingly became a determining factor in the internment process. Enemy aliens could be arrested and interned simply for acting in an "ugly and suspicious manner," a perception strengthened by their hapless appearance and dispirited demeanour. In a few cases internment proved useful in satisfying personal vendettas. Overwhelmingly, however, the spurious nature of arrests was the result of conjecture or prejudices borne of the belief that these people did not belong. The traditional role of police was to uphold the law and maintain order – now it included dealing with indolent foreigners with ascribed enemy loyalties who had no business being in the country.

Registration offices were set up in those municipalities where, it was felt, unemployed enemy aliens would gravitate in search of work and relief. By requiring them to report, officials could interrogate and scrutinize them on an ongoing basis, ascertaining whether they were able to maintain themselves. This provided a means for their control. But, for this to work, all enemy aliens within the designated areas would have to report. Yet the reality was that fewer registered than had been expected. This being worrisome, Order-in-Council PC 2721 was amended in November, a month after the original ordinance had been introduced, requiring registered enemy subjects to report more frequently and insisting on a more comprehensive pledge of loyalty. More immediately, policing intensified. Able to arrest and detain without restraint, police and militia increasingly approached those who were even remotely suspected of being enemy aliens, demanding evidence of their registration. If they failed to produce the necessary documentation, or if the documentation was incomplete, they were brought before a registrar or magistrate for processing. Indiscriminate arrests, including of naturalized citizens, resulted.

Although the registration bureaus were welcomed in the targeted cities, not everyone was satisfied. Resenting the presence of enemies throughout the country, the *Calgary Herald* declared that the steps taken were futile if not pointless. Nothing would come of monitoring the enemy alien since: "the fact of having to report once a week is no deterrent to a man determined to vent his spite on the enemies of his country."[35] Martial law, the *Herald* and like-minded voices maintained, was what was needed. This led to the idea that the military and police should be given a free hand in dealing with the problem, fortifying the militarized nature of the political environment.

Public talk of martial law, and more fundamentally the implementation of Order-in-Council PC 2721, had consequences. Cast in the role of enemy, the alien subject of Austro-Hungarian or German origin now faced the real and imminent possibility of being interned as a prisoner of war. Within this context, enemy aliens generally chose to comply with the registration order. Others, however, experiencing difficulties in finding and holding on to permanent work, ignored it. Indeed, for an enemy alien without work, the act of registering or reporting increasingly meant internment. The prospect of doing neither, therefore, seemed a better option. The result was predictable. The enemy alien who attempted to escape the attention of the authorities heightened the public's unease and suspicion. Unemployed enemy aliens were now understood to be not potential but real threats. Why else would they fail to register or report if not to bide their time and do harm? The immediate effect of having a public on alert was to increase the sense of wariness among the police and registrars, who now possessed the discretionary powers to arrest and intern.

Within this atmosphere of pronounced uncertainty, some enemy aliens attempted to pre-empt the process of registration by becoming naturalized, hoping that citizenship would afford them some protection. This resulted in an observable increase in the number of applicants who were long-term residents of the country. The rush towards acquiring citizenship did not go unnoticed, and the British Imperial Association of Toronto, for one, objected to the granting of naturalization to individuals of Austro-Hungarian origin and Germans during a war defined in imperial terms.[36] In the Canadian west, newspapers called for the naturalization of enemy subjects to be suspended altogether.

In response, the government sought to appease its critics by making the naturalization process more rigorous, requiring several individuals with standing in the community to vouch-safe for each applicant.[37] Multiple referees acting as guarantors in the naturalization process, however, failed to satisfy the more unyielding critics of the government. In Ottawa, objecting to enemy aliens applying for citizenship, several prominent community figures intervened in the local naturalization proceedings, arguing that the defence of the empire demanded their applications be precluded.[38] In Vancouver, Justice David Grant rejected multiple applicants on the basis of insufficient documentation, unapologetically declaring in the case of two ethnic Poles that: "[Since there was] a two-to-one chance of their being alien enemies, they would have to establish without a doubt they were not [enemy aliens] or their applications would be laid over until the peace is declared."[39] In British Columbia's East Kootenay district, Justice George Herbert Thompson refused to grant naturalization certificates to Austro-Hungarian and German applicants on the grounds that Canada was in a state of war and, as enemy subjects, "they had no status to apply for any civil rights in our courts."[40] These and other examples would highlight the idea that, being unwanted, they had no standing either before the law or the courts.

But it was the celebrated case of Professor P.W. Mueller, dismissed from his teaching position at the University of Toronto, that underscored the anti-alien undertone that had sidled its way into the judicial process. A resident of Canada for twenty years, but never naturalized, Mueller hoped that acquiring citizenship would enable him to be restored to his academic post at the university. When asked, "Whom do you want to win this war?" Mueller responded that this was a leading question and that it cast doubt on his loyalty and desire to become a citizen. He pointed out that he had nothing to do with the war and that the war had nothing to do with the process of becoming a Canadian citizen. The presiding judge rebuked the good professor, sharply retorting that the query was well within the purview of the court and it was not for him to question its reasoning. The judge asked again, "Do you want to see Britain victorious?" Mueller replied in the affirmative, only to have his application for naturalization rejected.[41]

For Mueller and others in a similar predicament, the prospect of acquiring citizenship through naturalization held out the promise that they might yet be protected from the suspicions and enmity directed at persons of enemy birth. It was a desperate strategy, which, in the end, proved futile. The process of identification and registration was skewed to ensure that, once they had been designated an enemy, an enemy they would remain. Isolated and without protection, aliens of enemy origin would be exposed to petty insults and rulings that would make their lives even more miserable and depressing. With nowhere to hide and nowhere to go, they endured the indignities of being identified as an enemy, all the while fearing that they would be arrested, interned, and made a POW under the security provisions of a country they called home.

The 15 August Royal Proclamation was initially conceived as a balance between security and rights. However, it failed in its very essence. Targeting a population on the basis of origin, the decree singled out a select class of individuals not to be trusted. Through negative inference – they could go about their business freely if they did not act on their foreign loyalties – the proclamation implied that immigrants of enemy nationality were actual enemies. This coloured the public's perception of the enemy alien, adding to the latter's difficult economic situation. It also helped frame the war measures used against these people. The war created the context in which security measures could be taken, while the deteriorating labour situation provided the immediate reason that they should be taken. But it was the Royal Proclamation that invoked the rationale for why and against whom such actions would be taken at all. There were presumed enemies in the land and precautions were needed.

What followed was Order-in-Council PC 2721 issued under the WMA. Its effect on the lives of enemy aliens was significant. There was, of course, the obligation to register and report, which arose from the perceived need to monitor and control the enemy alien population. But the ordinance was designed with more than traditional security in mind. It anticipated the management and control of the enemy alien by way of internment, and once it was accepted that this was needed, the process of arrest and detention rapidly expanded. This occurred because, when questioned, enemy aliens were obliged to answer whether or not they had the means to remain in Canada. Jobless and poor, they were likely candidates for internment. As part of a crude but broad surveillance system, they were brought before registrars, magistrates, or other officers of the Crown, and, once found to be indigent, made into POWs.

Security, of course, was cited as the rationale for internment, giving legitimacy to the measures. Yet the concept of internment was now so expanded as to make it virtually meaningless, a parody of the original idea and intent. But this could only have happened because of the perception that these individuals did not constitute part of the body politic. Both the Royal Proclamation and Order-in-Council PC 2721 ensured that this was so, casting them as outsiders. Once this occurred, and under the pressure of public opinion, the government's approach quickly took shape. For the government, internment served as a solution. For those targeted and unemployed, the probability was high that into the camps they would go.

Not fitting in, enemy aliens represented a certain type of risk. However, the danger they posed was less specific and more abstract. Given rising concerns about their presence in the country during a time of growing economic uncertainty and war, the issue was not just security but also identity. The way arrests were conducted, with wide latitude being granted police and registrars in their investigations, reinforced this point. The alien enemy did not belong. War simply hardened this understanding, which was made abundantly clear to those who, in their futile attempt to gain membership in the community, sought to become naturalized citizens.

Yet here they were, in Canada, having come voluntarily to the country with hope and promise. Moreover, the Canadian government had encouraged them to immigrate. It was the responsibility of the government, therefore, to determine how best to manage and even reconcile the seemingly irreconcilable. Since the difference between friend and enemy could not be successfully bridged, the government sought to avoid the impression that internment was punitive. Indeed, among certain officials, internment was even interpreted as a humane gesture that would save the unemployed enemy alien from the misery of poverty and hunger. But no matter how it was presented, there was no evading the obvious. Once designated enemy aliens, and given the ambient talk of war, they would be treated as individuals who were incompatible with the country's interests.

Not everyone was comfortable with this idea and the actions taken. They contended that the ill-conceived and potentially harmful measures used against enemy aliens had little to do with the country's security. They argued for common sense, empathy, and tolerance. Moreover, they insisted that those migrants who had made Canada their home and were affected by the vicissitudes of war needed to be reassured that their decision to settle was a good one – that the country was just and fair. As the *Manitoba Free Press* reasonably queried:

> While we are at war with Germany and Austria today and would misuse, persecute and deprive these people of their liberty while they are peaceably going about their business, what impression are we going to make on the rest of the world that is now at peace with us; yes, and even our Allies today? What guarantee have the people of Denmark, Norway, Sweden, Russia and the United States or any other country that perhaps in the near future we will be at war with, that their turn will be next to receive from our hands the same treatment as we are proposing to give to the Germans and Austrians now because we are at war with their countries?[42]

Only by considering the issue of their freedom and rights would a lasting, positive impression of Canada be created, giving credence to the idea that there was nothing to fear and much to admire in a place they would claim as their own. Only by assuring them that they were welcome, and that Canada was home, could some semblance of genuine security be had.

3

Enemy Alien Internment and the Blurring of the Military/Civilian Distinction

Rights, Treatment, Diplomacy

From 1914 to 1918, the introduction of military conscription and the rise of national armies culminated not only in the globalization of war but also in its radicalization. Mass mobilization placed civilians at the centre of war by highlighting their role as potential combatants. This transformed the nature of conflict in the twentieth century, levelling the distinction between combatant and non-combatant while challenging the normative, cultural boundaries that existed between the two.[1] As a result, the concept of enemy was reinterpreted to include civilians and entire nations. The enemy threat, vague and distant, was now seen as clear and imminent, and once brought into the conflict, civilians could not avoid its cruel reality.[2] Nevertheless, the devastating effects of a world at war gave rise to a compelling question: Was it still possible to lessen war's most egregious effects on civilians?

Foreshadowing the totality of war in the twentieth century, the 1907 Hague Convention (following the 1899 convention) tenuously set out terms that offered some protection to civilians. It held, for example, that civilians originating from enemy lands, if directly implicated in hostilities, could be interned as POWs. This meant that they possessed the limited rights extended to war prisoners or, at the very least, that they had the right "not to be exposed to worse treatment than their military counterparts."[3] The convention gave expression to the notion that, even in the darkness of war, civilized behaviour could be expected. Indeed, that enemy alien civilians who took up arms and were taken prisoner could be granted protection under the laws of war provided confidence that, at the very least, those not involved would neither be harmed nor interfered with as long as they were law-abiding. For immigrants, this was important. Encouraged to settle in Canada, yet made vulnerable by the conflict, the expectation was that their adopted home would exercise restraint.

However, with the onset of the Great War, nothing could either still suspicious minds or lessen the grip that the culture of war had on society.[4] The belief that the threat was immediate and far-reaching marked as foes those who could trace their origins to enemy lands. Mass mobilization as part of modern warfare reinforced this attitude. Accordingly, these everyday immigrants, living through the turmoil of war and dealing with the contradiction of having been invited as settlers to Canada, yet now being under suspicion, faced a series of important questions. What did the concept of enemy alien mean in the context of modern war? Were they subjects beholden to an enemy sovereign or simply civilians in their adopted country? Further, if they did not engage in hostile acts, could the fact that Canada was at war still result in their internment as POWs? And, if so, under what circumstances?[5]

Central to their predicament in Canada were the increasingly difficult economic conditions at the beginning of the war, which led to distinctions being made between the native-born and the immigrant – namely, those citizens without means but who warranted support versus those who were seen as less deserving because of their foreign origins. Conflict magnified this difference. The difficulty was not simply that these migrants were jobless but, rather, they were now classified as individuals of enemy birth. With implied enemy allegiances because of their birth origins, they were soon seen as constituting a risk. Although compassion intimated that they were civilians and mercy might be extended to them, it was also the case that these people were now effectively deemed adversaries. A dilemma was presented. Could the perception that they were enemies be reconciled with the fact that, having nothing to do with the war, they were blameless and therefore deserving of consideration and assistance?

In South Africa and India, at the turn of the century, the British created internment camps in order to conduct sanitary surveillance and social control during periods of famine, pestilence, and conflict.[6] Being an expression both of Britain's interest in imposing order and discipline on its colonial frontiers and the liberal impulse to provide relief through quarantine against disease and starvation, internment camps often had contradictory objectives. The camps served simultaneously as places of detention and refuge.[7] In Canada, this dualism found its way into the rationale behind internment. Although regarded as places of forcible confinement, camps across the country were also seen as havens, where work could be provided to those who were without.

But what did this mean for civilians in Canada who were interned as POWs and in whose persons the distinction between combatant and non-combatant – soldier and civilian – was now blurred? How were they to be treated? Moreover, what effect did this have internationally and what did it say about the law of nations and the dictates of public conscience at a time when humanity was being tested? Given the implications for those who languished behind barbed wire, and the bewildering set of circumstances that confronted innocent settlers who called Canada home during a time of great upheaval, these were crucial questions.

In August 1915, while travelling by motorcar to the military training camp at Petawawa in northern Ontario, the governor general's adjutant, Lieutenant Colonel Edward Stanton, observed teams of men with picks and shovels, labouring away, making improvements to the road under the supervision of soldiers. He was informed that those working under military guard were enemy aliens interned at the nearby training facility, which also served as an internment camp. This came as a surprise to him as he believed this sort of activity was proscribed. He conveyed his concern in the form of an inquiry to Canada's acting undersecretary of state, W.H. Walker. Walker responded that adverse economic conditions had forced the Canadian government to intern enemy aliens as POWs and to put them to work, adding that the government had no recourse. Stanton was told that, since these individuals had "to be supported by the authorities of Canada, the status of prisoners of war and the regulations governing their custody and maintenance [were] accorded and applied to these unfortunate aliens of enemy nationality who necessarily became a public charge."[8]

At issue was the economic downturn at the start of the war that resulted in large numbers of enemy aliens being dismissed from employment. In the tense atmosphere of uncertainty augmented by the conflict, with questions of duty and loyalty quickly taking shape, it was felt that enemy aliens were not to be cossetted. Under a special ordinance introduced under the War Measures Act, enemy aliens who lacked the means to remain in the country were to be interned as POWs and put to work. The practice of interning civilians was not unknown. During the late nineteenth and early twentieth centuries, Britain used internment as a catchall to address a series of challenges on its colonial frontier, a precedent that indirectly shaped the Canadian experience.[9] Still, the way it was conceived in Canada – a security measure first introduced as a precaution but then broadened to deal with the problem of enemy alien unemployment – raised concerns about its lawfulness.

A matter of political discussion followed Stanton's inquiry. The deputy minister of justice, Edmund Newcombe, stubbornly defended the government's position, arguing that the aim of internment was to afford "some occupation for people who must necessarily, in the interest of humanity, be maintained at the public expense" and that "neither the state of war nor any rule sanctioned by international convention or practice require[d] that destitute people of any nationality, when seeking relief from the State, should be immune from a similar requirement."[10] Newcombe was convinced that interning these people as POWs was not illegal since doing so enabled them to work on projects for which they were "qualified." Moreover, since they were unemployed, homeless, and penniless, Canada was justified in putting them to work not only because as POWs this was allowed but it was also in keeping with domestic practice, which saw paupers and vagrants work in exchange for relief.[11] The point of the exercise was to have these people engaged in productive labour.

Newcombe's argument embodied several competing ideas that he sought to reconcile. For the indigent to be put to work, they had to be identified and interned as POWs. This was justified because it was believed that this would alleviate their distress. But could civilians be interned as war prisoners because they lacked jobs, as the deputy minister claimed? That the government's position was problematic became apparent when an application was referred to the judge advocate general requesting that a district court martial be convened against two internees at Kingston's Fort Henry who had been caught trying to escape by breaking through the fortress's stone wall. The judge refused the application principally on the grounds that the men were not POWs but interned civilians.[12] Since they were civilians, this suggested that the framework sanctioning their treatment as war prisoners was incompatible with their status in law. The opinion of the military judge compelled the director of internment, Major General William Otter, to seek clarification from the minister of justice, fearing, as he did, that "we may be acting illegally."[13]

Newcombe, citing the 1914 *Manual of Military Law*, replied that, having been apprehended and interned for "military reasons," internees were not civilians but war prisoners.[14] Insofar as they were defined as subjects of an enemy sovereign liable to mobilization,

Newcombe's explanation made sense. Yet, being across the ocean and far away from their homelands, the vast majority of enemy aliens were removed from the horror that was the First World War. Moreover, as immigrants, they were keen to convey that Canada was now their home, the place where they would raise their families. Newcombe thought otherwise. Birthright inferred that their loyalties lay elsewhere, which precluded them from having any special claim on Canada.[15] In Newcombe's estimation, enemy aliens could and would be lawfully interned as POWs. As for those interned, they were owed little and would be dealt with as seen fit.

Not everyone agreed. In a petition to the king's representative in Canada (the governor general), internees at the Vernon internment camp outlined their principal grievances. As they were civilians who had been rendered vulnerable by war, Canada, they argued, had both a political and a moral obligation to protect them. Since they had followed the government's official rulings and orders, their rights should not have been suspended. In doing so, the government, they maintained, had exposed them to arbitrary arrest and internment – not because of something they did but because of who they were.

In principle, the presence of law keeps the dark impulses of society at bay while its absence allows for their manifestation. This belief, the Vernon internees declared, was at the heart of their misfortune. By exposing them to nativist pique, by failing to shield them from unfounded allegations, the government had made it possible for them to be interned as POWs. This, they argued, was Canada's failure and shame: "In the case of nearly all of us, we were deprived of our liberty for no other reason than just because we were Germans. [S]ince no proof of guilt was required against us, suspicion, however unfounded, sufficed. [I]t was a welcome for many, who owed us money, wanted our farms, or thought they had a grievance against us to denounce us as pro-German in order to escape the necessity of paying their debts or getting a cheap, but powerfully effective revenge for their supposed grievances."[16]

Highlighting the radicalizing nature of modern war, the security question became racialized. Under such conditions, even the most innocuous behaviour of the enemy alien gave rise to suspicion and alarm. Indeed, from the very start of the war, rumours and denunciations proliferated, elevating the public's anxiety and disquiet over their presence in the country.[17] Scheming enemy aliens were thought to be everywhere, biding their time, waiting for the right moment to strike. That they would attack was a forgone conclusion since it was assumed that their inclination was to be loyal to the country of their birth.

What happened next stemmed from the belief that, in the context of war and economic uncertainty, such people had to be controlled. Following a process of mandatory registration, enemy aliens were required to report to designated local officials. Those who did not comply, or found in violation of any order-in-council, were at once arrested and interned. But so, too, were those discovered to be indigent and without work (a group that was increasingly targeted for internment). To avoid arrest, some took to crossing the border; others hid, nestling within their communities.[18] Not everyone could do so, as the hundreds and then thousands of interned would attest.

All of this occurred because war had transformed those who could trace their origins to enemy lands into much-maligned figures who were to be feared and reviled. The truth of the matter , however, was that these people were settlers who had been invited to the country. More important, they were civilians. Still, viewed as a problem that needed to be dealt with, and having no protection, they were liable to being interned as POWs. No matter how inconceivable this seemed, it was only to be expected once the government deemed it necessary. But what did it mean to be a civilian interned as a prisoner of war and what were the implications?

For Canadian officials, the POW designation was important because it allowed for the internment of enemy aliens and under certain conditions the lawful sanctioning of the state's use of their labour. Thus, as war prisoners, internees were expected to work but, under the laws of war, only for their own benefit and only if they volunteered to do so. This meant, among other things, that they could not be compelled to work. Yet the unfolding rationale behind internment – the joblessness of the enemy alien – implied that they would work. So, what if they refused? How then might the government put them to work without violating the international rules governing POWs? And what of the laws of war pertaining to interned civilians (an entirely different category) and their treatment while imprisoned? What did international jurisprudence have to say on the matter?

On the treatment of captured combatants as POWs the Hague Convention was clear, but on the treatment of interned civilians it was vague.[19] Nevertheless, because the internment of enemy alien civilians was being widely practised among states, it became a pressing issue.[20] Prior to the First World War, it was unforeseen that enemy aliens would be interned in large numbers. And although there were international provisions regarding the internment of irregulars, including insurrectionists, saboteurs, and spies, there was little guidance regarding the application of a policy that would see civilian enemy aliens being interned broadly and systematically. This lack of guidance proved significant.

Indeed, in Canada, the ambiguous status of interned enemy aliens allowed for the widest interpretation of the law, making it possible for them to be put to work. It was argued, for example, that there was nothing prohibiting the unemployed and indigent from being deployed on public projects since domestic law already provided for this. Implied was the idea that internees were civilians. Yet, characterizing them as such did not vitiate their standing as POWs. They continued to be considered war prisoners because this justified their initial internment and sanctioned their use as labour under specific conditions. But it was their standing as civilians that allowed for them to be forcibly put to work because the protection extended to traditional POWs did not apply; after all, they had not been captured on the field of battle. This combination of being considered both civilian internees and war prisoners – no matter how much in tension – had implications. Thousands of destitute and homeless enemy aliens were immediately arrested and interned as POWs, lending cover to the goal of authorizing their work. But it was their status as interned civilians – individuals without fully established rights – that ensured there would be no impediment to compelling them to work.

The internment sites created in the wilderness of the Canadian frontier saw unemployed and impoverished enemy alien civilians forced to work under military watch. Meanwhile, the organization of these facilities as labour camps served as a rejoinder to the criticism that internment would become "a lazy man's haven."[21] This helped placate a clamorous public that was demanding enemy aliens competing for jobs be removed from public sight. Enemy aliens represented a liability, and for the native-born Canadian population the argument was basic: these people had made their way into the country and now, being unwanted, Canada had to be rid of them. Or, at the very least, they had to be sent to internment camps in the Canadian wilderness to "work out their anti-British spleen upon good, tough Canadian stumps."[22]

In keeping with public opinion and the government's political direction, the prisoners were compelled to work. But there were other extenuating circumstances that enabled the policy and practice of internment to unfold as it did. From the start of the war, it was evident that internment would be a costly affair. Large numbers of individuals were being processed. The shortage of space in existing military prisons and provincial jails, as well as the decision to have enemy aliens put to work, led to several innovations. To lessen the financial burden of their incarceration, partnerships were formed between internment operations, provincial governments, railway companies, and dominion ministries, including the Department of Militia and Defence and the Department of Interior's parks branch, with terms negotiated regarding cost sharing, division of responsibilities, and the creation of internment camps at sites that met the needs of the contracting parties.

The new partners appreciated the opportunity that the use of prisoners presented. However, as partners, they also insisted on value for money. Thus, the internees were deployed where they could be used most productively: refurbishing military facilities and training grounds, constructing roads in the interior of British Columbia and the national parks, clearing land for colonization in northern Ontario and Quebec, and repairing railway lines in Atlantic Canada and on the prairies. Economic interests soon dictated the prisoners' work schedules and treatment. Careful supervision by project overseers, hired by the partners, ensured that quotas would be met, expenditures justified, and payments accounted for.[23]

Since the partnering agencies were responsible for paying POW wages, the failure of internment authorities to deliver on time and according to schedule became a constant source of tension and disagreement. The disputes periodically resulted in threats to cancel contracts. Consequently, commandants and officers were under inordinate pressure to adhere to schedules and quotas, underscoring the importance of maintaining discipline. The camps' military administrators were pressured by the project managers to ignore or adjust the military rules governing the treatment of POWs in order to expedite the work. Meanwhile, prisoner resistance was met with a variety of coercive measures, including punitive diets, solitary confinement, and beatings.

Guided by economic criteria, the security aspect of the operation, which had informed the original policy, was soon undercut. As a result, prisoners came to be viewed not as combatants with rights but as enemies against whom the use of coercion and abuse became the norm. The prisoners lodged complaints, demanding a stop to their mistreatment. Where these failed, defiance was commonly expressed in the form of work stoppages, hunger strikes, and riots. There were also escapes, some of which ended badly. Six internees were fatally shot, adding to the list of internment camp fatalities – 107 in total – which included those who succumbed to injuries, ailments, and mental despair brought on by isolation and suffering.

In blurring the civilian military distinction, those who were interned had no way of avoiding their fate. Indeed, they were used unreservedly, giving credence to the idea that they were a prize of war. As one guard would later explain: "Anybody who asked [us] to do anything, we provided the slaves."[24] The description was clearly overdrawn, but the underlying sentiment was not. These were individuals who did not belong and to whom nothing was owed. In this regard, internment operations received numerous requests for the use of internees as a source of cheap labour. In an effort to enhance local tourism and open the region to settlement, the citizens of Nakusp in the BC interior petitioned, unsuccessfully, for prisoners from the Vernon internment camp to build a road to connect their community to the nearby mineral hot springs.[25] Similarly, Nova Scotia's commissioner for public works made an unsuccessful bid to requisition prisoners for the purpose of building roads in and around Halifax and Dartmouth.[26]

These and other requests reflected the country's general mood, especially after German atrocities in Europe (both real and alleged) were widely reported in the press. Capable of conducting outrages overseas, it stood to reason that all enemy aliens in the country – seen as no less savage in character than their overseas kindred – should be interned and conscripted as forced labour. Thus, public calls for the mass conscription of enemy alien labour became more frequent and widespread. Although this demand was hard to ignore, officials resisted – not because it was wrong but, as one senior official noted, given the scale of such an operation, it was simply impossible to carry out.[27]

Not everyone, however, was comfortable with the use of civilians as forced labour or with the conditions under which they worked. British Columbia's deputy minister for public works, J.E. Griffith, acknowledged that austerity measures introduced by the internment administration as a cost-cutting exercise (e.g., reducing meat rations) were adversely affecting the health of prisoners. Engaged in heavy, manual work, the prisoners complained of hunger and exhaustion. He threatened to cancel the projects to which they had been contracted "unless they were fed like human beings."[28] Still, Griffith was not entirely dissuaded from using the labour of the prisoners, nor was he concerned about how it was obtained. The benefits overruled any misgivings he might have had. In correspondence with the director of the internment operations, he observed: "We are not unmindful of the fact that we have had the opportunity of obtaining cheap labour, but we would have liked to make the best use of it."[29] Griffith would not be disappointed: interned enemy aliens would be forced to work until there was a change in policy.

Notwithstanding the Canadian position, which blurred the military/civilian distinction, Germany, receiving diplomatic reports on those imprisoned, concluded that they were being treated as conventional POWs. Interned enemy aliens, however, were civilians, not captured military combatants and as such needed to be treated with greater consideration than personnel seized on the field of battle. This was a principle that Germany was prepared to defend and from which it would not retreat, following, as it did, from the German law relating to imperial citizenship that held that Germans overseas remained subjects of the emperor.[30] To the degree that their civilian status as internees was not fully recognized, Berlin looked to protect its subjects abroad.

But it was more than that. A major impetus behind Germany's obligation to defend its nationals overseas was the political manoeuvring between Britain and Germany regarding the treatment of those interned. Allegations of German misdeeds were widespread in the British and Allied press. And although Berlin's objections were disingenuous – certainly after the deportation of Belgian and French civilians to Germany as forced labour in 1916 – it was nevertheless important that Berlin counter reports of German barbarity and inhumanity by pointing out irregularities in the British handling of interned enemy aliens.[31] The camps in Canada became a point of interest in Germany's efforts to offset British allegations of brutality.

The principal claim in German diplomatic protests related to the growing evidence of the use of interned civilians as forced labour. The accusation was prompted by American diplomatic reports. Kapuskasing and Spirit Lake, in northern Ontario and Quebec, were singled out as internment facilities where, it was reported, German civilian internees were forcibly required to fell trees and clear land. Germany demanded the British government instruct Canadian officials to put a stop to this activity. It was further communicated that, if the situation remained unadjusted, the German government would be justified in taking countermeasures against British subjects interned in Germany.[32]

The threat could not be ignored. Ottawa responded by arguing that its efforts were aimed at relieving the distress of those no longer able to provide for themselves.[33] Moreover, citing Article 6 of the Annex to the Fourth Hague Convention, authorities claimed that Canada could employ the labour of POWs according to their rank and status, thus authorizing their work on public projects. They further insisted that the prisoners were not compelled to work but, rather, did so voluntarily, and were clothed and fed at government expense, receiving twenty-five cents a day for their labour in accordance with the international regulations governing the treatment of POWs. The explanation and provisos, however, convinced Germany that Canadian authorities did not consider the internees to be civilians. As such, the internees were working under conditions that did not apply.[34] German objections were now increasingly accompanied by threats of retaliation, which became more sinister after allegations regarding the abuse of German internees at the Amherst and Nanaimo camps became public.[35]

With British captives in German hands, reprisals were of concern to London.[36] In view of the escalating nature of German protests, Britain pressured Canada into accepting the principle that those interned were not POWs in the conventional sense; rather, they were civilians. In keeping with Britain's imperial lead, Canada reluctantly obliged, but with a twist. The notion that these people were civilians was accepted because it lent itself to the domestic understanding that vagrants could be made to work in exchange for relief. Still, under the WMA, enemy aliens were interned as POWs. So, to reconcile the contradiction of their status, the internees, whose identities alternated separately and as needed between civilians and POWs, were now simply identified as "civilian POWs." The designation proved useful. By utilizing this hybrid, for which there was no clear international understanding, the uncertainty surrounding the treatment of the internees was reinforced, enabling them to be deployed on work projects regardless of the protests.

Importantly, because there was no international ruling regarding how civilian POWs were to be treated, Canada, in keeping with its interests, was left to pursue its own course of action. When, in February 1916, the minister of the interior responded to an opposition inquiry in Canada's Parliament, acknowledging that the nature of the work in the camps was coerced because this was the only way to get anything done, Bonar Law, the UK colonial secretary, on learning of the news, demanded to know how this could be reconciled "with the assurance that ha[d] been given to the German Government that no civilian prisoner [was] compelled to work."[37] What the colonial secretary failed to understand was that, at this stage, putting unemployed enemy aliens to work was the whole point of Canadian internment.

Several neutral American representatives who had been sent at the behest of Germany to investigate alluded to the continuing use of interned civilians as forced labour. The internees were widely employed on a variety of projects, and, given the scope of the operation, there was no ignoring it. The evidence was everywhere and in full view. Still, even though those interned were clearly civilians, US reports side-stepped the issue, derisively commenting that, as common labourers, they were already habituated to the work and as a result not excessively burdened.[38] The reports reaffirmed the belief that this was their lot in life and they had no reason for complaint.

As for the allegations of mistreatment reported in foreign press accounts, internment officials in Canada addressed these as they arose, frequently rejecting them as fabrications or gross exaggerations (including the accusation that internees were sent as penal battalions into the wilderness where they were forced to work until exhausted). Not every allegation, however, could be easily dismissed. Ongoing complaints of abuse and mistreatment – unwittingly corroborated by incriminating statements made by camp officers – punctuated the reports of US consular officials. Some were trivialized, while other more serious charges, such as excessive discipline, punishment, and unprovoked beatings, required explanation. Where the evidence proved incontrovertible, Canadian officials explained what adjustments had been made.[39]

In the main, officials felt that they were doing all they could to ensure that, at the very least, the operation was being run according to the provisions and guidelines set out in the military manual and various army acts. They could also take comfort in the reports of some American representatives who praised the internment authorities for providing for the health, hygiene, and general well-being of the prisoners.[40] Others, however, who were less inclined to suspend judgment regarding what amounted to the unjust imprisonment and forced labour of civilians, criticized the operation.

US consul Gebhard Willrich, for one, tasked with reporting on conditions at Spirit Lake in November 1916 after prisoner protests were clandestinely made known to him, was not impressed when he visited the camp.[41] Willrich was surprised by what he observed and learned. Huddled together in shacks that scarcely sheltered them from the cold and harsh weather, and deprived of rations because they had refused to work, the internees were in a wretched physical state. Also in evidence was the contempt with which officers and soldiers held the enemy alien, the prisoners complaining of beatings, solitary confinement, insults, and neglect. A sense of hopelessness and despair prevailed. A few of them stated that they no longer cared what happened, refusing to obey orders despite being punished.

From Willrich's perspective, it was incredible that ordinary, innocent people could be treated this way. The problem, he argued, was that these were civilians who demonstrated neither disloyalty nor hostility towards the country. Moreover, by adopting Canada as their new home, they had demonstrated a commitment to the country. Now, however, they were regarded as "quasi-criminals." In his opinion, this was against the best interests of the country. He found it incomprehensible that the government could believe that its sordid treatment of these people was somehow to its advantage. But Willrich's job as a diplomat was to report, and not opine on Canadian government policy. Willrich was soon relieved of his post at the request of Canada's undersecretary of state for external affairs after the latter received a copy of the diplomat's report and registered a protest with Washington.

Willrich objected to the coerced nature of internee labour, but this was nothing new. A long-standing criticism of Canadian internment policy was that internees were being compelled to work. Although Canadian officials continued to hold that this was not the case, Germany, ever watchful, persisted in its demand that under no circumstances should German civilians in the camps be forced to labour.[42] In the end, however, neither German resolve nor threats mattered; rather, in 1917, the remaining internees' refusal to work (they conducted strikes despite the pressure brought to bear on them) and industry's mounting appetite for labour inexorably led to the parole of the internees, at least those who were viewed as docile and non-threatening.

For those considered obstinate, quarrelsome, and truculent, as well as for the infirm and insane, a different fate awaited. They would remain behind barbed wire well after hostilities had ceased in 1918 and a peace treaty was concluded. Deemed unfit as prospective citizens, a thousand or more were deported, among whom were scores of labour activists and progressives arrested and interned as "undesirables" during the postwar labour troubles. Mustered onto European-bound ships and released on arrival, they made their way back to their ancestral homes as best they could. Representing a sad ending to a difficult story, the deportations served as an exclamation point. War reduced them to enemies, the coming of peace rendered them disposable.

The unconditional nature of the First World War ensured that it would be a novel undertaking. The rubric "necessity of war" was invoked to validate all sorts of measures and actions. It came as no surprise that few would be spared, giving the First World War its modern meaning.[43] But the idea that war should be conducted on a higher plane – that there were rights that had to be respected and norms followed – also formed part of the modern calculus. Prefiguring the extent and scale of the violence to come, diplomacy insisted that the viciousness of war be somehow curtailed, if not contained. But could the conflicting impulses behind doing what was right as opposed to doing what was necessary be reconciled?

The incompatibility of these political priorities made for difficult and often confused policy choices. In Canada, the internment of immigrants who came from enemy lands was one choice. On its face, this choice reflected the country's nativist bent, which demanded the removal of the undeserving immigrant from the ranks of Canada's employed. More deeply, it acknowledged the dictates of political necessity by factoring in the impact of imperial sentiment and public opinion on the wider war effort.[44] However, interning enemy aliens was also a choice that demanded adherence, at least nominally, to the requirements of natural justice and the rule of law. To the degree that Canada was aware of its duties and responsibilities, both as an international actor and ally, there was no escaping its obligations. In the context of modern war, therefore, it fell to political leadership to somehow navigate these competing claims.

Among other things, the novel nature of modern war involved the radical reconceptualization of who was considered a participant. Modern war broke down old distinctions and created new hierarchies based on identity, race and class, shaping the conduct of war in new and unexpected ways.[45] This redefinition of who was a participant would guide Canada's internment policy. Specifically, immigrants viewed as subjects of states at war with Canada would be made out to be alien enemies, leading to their internment as POWs. But this decision turned on its head the traditional meaning and purpose of internment. Security measures now applied to an expanded category of participant, thereby transforming internment into a political instrument that proved useful in dealing with thousands of impoverished enemy aliens and, later, political and labour activists.

Internment was noteworthy in that it authorized the labour of immigrants who came from enemy lands as POWs. Native-born Canadians and "friendly aliens" – immigrants from allied nations – were no less affected by the difficult economic situation in Canada. Yet internment provided a solution to the central problem posed by the enemy alien demographic – namely, their poverty and joblessness. Still, the policy of putting internees to work as war prisoners carried with it certain liabilities. Under the laws of war, POWs could work but not be compelled to do so. Did this, however, not defeat the purpose of internment? The conundrum was squared by acknowledging (within limits) the prisoners' civilian status. Since the conventions of war were conspicuously silent on the rights of civilians as POWs, they would be forced to work, and those who resisted could be coerced. All of this highlighted the fact that they did not belong, and, in the camps, they were made to understand this hard lesson.

Despite the diplomatic wrangling and equivocation regarding the status of interned enemy aliens and the issue of work, all the warring parties understood the need for some semblance of standards. Germany, in attempting to protect its co-nationals abroad, argued that, because the laws of war recognized combatants' rights, these same rights, at minimum, should have applied to civilian internees. However, because these prisoners were non-combatants but, rather, civilians, Germany maintained they were entitled to even greater rights. Either way, Canada was at a political disadvantage, and German officials, recognizing the propaganda value, would not let go. Much of this, of course, was fraught with irony given Germany's own disreputable record of misconduct towards the civilians it interned in the occupied territories of Europe. But this was war, and the propaganda advantage useful.

The principle of humanitarian protection, of course, was just and right. After all, interned enemy aliens were civilians. The internees at the Vernon camp who petitioned the governor general understood this, arguing that they were migrants uninvolved in the war. Committed to Canada, their contention was that they were deserving of respect and protection. What they encountered – the fact that there was no place for them in the country because of who they were – was a rude awakening, resulting in a sense of betrayal. Meanwhile, Canadian officials repeatedly claimed that the decision to intern these people was taken out of necessity. This explanation, however, was a travesty, failing as it did to acknowledge Canada's responsibility to provide fair treatment to those who would settle the country but were made vulnerable by war. It further failed to recognize that they were civilians whose status needed to be acknowledged, respected, and protected. As the experience of internment in Canada would demonstrate, the moral imperative to do what was right was ignored, pointing to the suborning nature of modern war, which obscured the civilian/military distinction and made enemies of those whom Canada had invited to its shores.

4

"Get Out and Stay Out"

British Columbia and the Social-Political Dynamics of the Enemy Alien Issue

In August 1914, much of the population of Canada greeted news of the start of the Great War with enthusiasm. Tens of thousands, eager to participate, hurriedly sought to enlist. The fervour was not entirely unexpected, being, as it was, an expression of Canada's place in the British imperial fold. Indeed, imperialism, as the prevailing ideology, obviated any need for an explanation of why British rule and civilization needed defending.[1] To be a British subject was to be an imperial citizen, standing as one with the motherland. Thus, with the metropole under attack, unflinching patriotism and belief in British right and civilization galvanized the martial spirit in much of Canada.

The idea of "King and Empire" was deeply felt, featuring in Canada's political identity.[2] This included British Columbia, where the colonial imprint was profoundly embedded. The effect was to impress upon the majority in the province the importance of embracing hard and fast distinctions relating to loyalty – an attitude that intensified when Ottawa introduced emergency security measures – controlling those in the country with perceived dubious loyalties. Consequently, in addition to the patriotism that rallied the faithful in British Columbia, there was a strong undercurrent of suspicion and wariness regarding those originating from enemy lands and whose foreign allegiances were presumed – the enemy alien. Guarding against threats from within was as important as the fight overseas: it was part of the wider struggle.[3]

With divisions in place, defending the existing order was straightforward. Yet the distrust of the enemy alien was tempered by the notion that immigrants were still needed both to power industry and work the land. This would highlight the essential contradiction in the relationship. The present order had to be protected against those who might threaten it while, simultaneously, accepting that those same people helped sustain it. How, then, was this paradox to be addressed practically?

In British Columbia, as elsewhere in the country, the question involved public opinion – the barometer by which acceptance of the enemy alien would be measured. To the degree that their role and place in society had to be delineated, it fell to the press to explain who they were and what they represented. Editorials, as a result, were frequently crafted around basics: differences, for example, in culture, values, and behaviour. But public opinion also needed to be guided, and this offered the press a more robust role. Accordingly, the press framed and clarified those issues that mattered most during wartime, directing readers how to think critically about the enemy alien.[4]

Certain questions loomed large. Security, to be sure, but also the indefinite place of the immigrant in Canadian society. Serving as yardsticks, these questions brought attention to other important issues: the nexus between identity and loyalty, the purpose and function of internment, and, later, the future of immigration. No less important was the responsibility and duty of governments. By raising these matters, newspapers served as purveyors of information vital not only to the security of the country but also its prospects. To this end, with empire and civilization as the lens through which these issues were examined and assessed, British Columbians and other Canadians were asked: Upon what foundations would the country be built? Who belonged or did not belong? And what measures should government take?

These questions connected the individual and different levels of governments to broader points of national and even international importance. They were also linked to local concerns such as employment, welfare, and the ability of political representatives to grasp the gravity of the moment. Governments, as a result, were urged to do more and exercise greater diligence. Thus, the importance of dealing with enemy aliens as a problem was highlighted, as was the role that internment could play in addressing it. However, for this to happen, the standing of the enemy alien as both a social and a political liability had to be clearly articulated, and any reservations about the country's obligations toward them had to be quashed. To this end, the press in British Columbia pushed to ensure that the right conclusions were drawn and the public was sufficiently mobilized to pressure governments and politicians, especially if they were lagging in interest or commitment. This dynamic of press, public opinion, and government would shape the debate surrounding the enemy alien.

Throughout, the press used its influence to connect with wider suspicions pertaining to the problem and perceived threat posed by enemy aliens. This resonated with public opinion in BC, where imperial identity and patriotic feelings ran strong.[5] However, because members of the public were already primed to suspect those who might prove to be a danger, minimum effort was required to persuade them that the problem was real. Nevertheless, focus was needed to ensure that the government would act more forcefully, and to this end BC newspapers obliged by guiding the faithful towards increased vigilance.

On the cusp of a world marching towards war in 1914, globalization imbued the pending conflict with a particular meaning. It would not be just a struggle for territory, power, or influence; rather, assigned moral meaning and weight, it would be cast as a war to preserve civilization. As a result, victory would be calculated not only in terms of spoils but also of the triumph of British civilization, which was assumed to be in the right. In an age defined by imperialism, where the parties to the conflict would seek to gain political advantage, this was to be expected. Indeed, the conflict between the British and German Empires was as much a question of cultural supremacy and vindication as of military victory.[6]

In British Columbia, where British authority and influence were intertwined with imperial identity, the struggle on the frontier meant protecting the province's character as a bastion of Britannic influence and rule.[7] However, as an "inherently brittle construct," the imperial idea in Canada needed constant replenishing and reinforcement.[8] This meant not only burnishing the history and myths of the British Empire but also drawing attention to the ethno-cultural character of the imperial project.[9] By emphasizing this dimension, a clear distinction was made between those who could fully participate in the project and those who could only be marginal to it. This distinction proved useful during wartime, when issues of identity were magnified. Thus, BC residents of German origin were publicly cast in the role of enemy despite, prior to the conflict, having been recognized as upstanding citizens and kindred colonizing spirits.[10] Their marginalization was reinforced by the government's promulgation of the Royal Proclamation and the War Measures Act, which outlined the controls that were to be imposed on unnaturalized German immigrants and other enemy subjects.

Predictably, suspicions regarding enemy alien motives quickly proliferated. Speculation soon gave rise to rumours. The BC press, for example, gave full play to stories of a planned German attack on Canada by German Americans from Washington state.[11] These accounts served as a reminder of the potential domestic danger: Germany could succeed only if it received assistance from within. Consequently, press descriptions of suspected spy activity in Vancouver's Stanley Park and purported enemy wireless communication in South Vancouver amplified the public's anxiety about the enemy alien. Reports of strong pro-German sympathies among German immigrants in both Canada and the United States were also worrisome. Therefore, when a provincial Department of Alien Reservists was hastily organized, both to prevent the departure of enemy aliens for the US and to deal with suspect enemy aliens in British Columbia, the public enthusiastically welcomed the news.[12]

Still, the more immediate concern was the country's perilous position given the presence of so many enemy aliens. In a conflict increasingly defined by its civilizational character – underscored by ongoing reports of German cruelty towards civilians in occupied Belgium and France – the role and place of the enemy alien in Canada and the province specifically were problematic. What was to be done with them? An impassioned letter-writer to the *Vancouver Sun* advocated that resident Germans in Canada be used as hostages and shot as retribution for atrocities committed by the German military in Europe. For the editors of the *Vancouver Sun*, this proposal – "no doubt made in good faith" – was a step too far.[13] Nevertheless, the newspaper noted that enemy aliens did represent a problem. The economy was in crisis, and many British Columbians found themselves unemployed. Should assistance be extended to those considered adversaries, the editorials asked? When a terrible toll was being exacted on Canadians fighting overseas, did not helping the enemy at home represent a betrayal? In the context of war, a fine line existed between mercy and folly. Being hardnosed was not only prudent but also patriotic.[14]

With unemployment on the rise, the desperate situation of the enemy alien did not elicit much public sympathy. Still, the prospect of bread riots could not be entirely ignored. A disorderly mob, demanding food, had rocked the city of Seattle in neighbouring Washington state. Fearing the same in Vancouver, city officials increased relief to the destitute, including enemy aliens. But municipal officials also looked to other levels of government and welcomed any measures that could improve the situation.

Although the majority of the 850 Austro-Hungarians in Vancouver were said to be "indifferent to the war," when Ottawa issued special Order-in-Council PC 2721 under the War Measures Act, allowing enemy aliens to be interned and put to work as prisoners of war, this was positively received, as were reports about the creation of large internment camps in the province. Equally reassuring was the news about the merging of the province's Department of Alien Reservists with the newly established Internment Directorate with its security mandate. So, too, was the transfer of the provincial prison facilities in Nanaimo and Vernon (where scores of enemy aliens were interned at the start of the war) to dominion jurisdiction. With Ottawa and the province finally taking the matter seriously, the press, to the relief of readers, could report that the problem of enemy aliens was finally being addressed – and none too soon given the extent of joblessness among the hungry foreign-born.[15]

Creating an internment system that potentially involved thousands of enemy aliens would prove challenging. The problem of finances was especially concerning, and it prompted a search for partners. In late 1914 and early 1915, after negotiating with the Department of Militia and Defence, the Department of Interior's Parks Branch, and the governments of Quebec and Ontario, internment officials planned for several new internment camps. The BC government also conferred with the Internment Directorate regarding the creation of an internment camp for unemployed enemy aliens in the province's interior. The partners were to help underwrite the operational costs of internment in exchange for POW labour.

In British Columbia, there was some urgency about getting on with a plan. Hunger in Vancouver during late winter and early spring stretched local efforts to assist the poor.[16] In April, when it became apparent that the proposed internment camp for British Columbia's interior would be delayed, angry city officials responded, seeking to pressure the province and Ottawa by discontinuing local aid. This was an unfortunate decision as panic soon set in among the enemy alien population. A group of enemy aliens, marching to the American consulate, appealed for assistance but, upon turning disorderly, were dispersed by police. The press denounced the lot of them as "spongers" living off the goodwill of the city. Arguing they should be "placed in detention camps and put to work on the roads," the press demanded that Ottawa act on Order-in-Council PC 2721 by carrying through with its intention to intern and force the enemy aliens in the province to work as POWs.[17]

The disturbance in Vancouver had displaced the original proposal of the Internment Directorate to create a new internment camp in the province's interior (delayed because overcrowding at facilities in Quebec and Ontario had prioritized the creation of additional camps in these jurisdictions). Still, the trouble in Vancouver was unsettling, and, with the press calling for action, the provincial government took immediate steps. At the direction of the BC premier, a special grant of $10,000 was allocated to assist with relief efforts in the city. More important, instructions were issued to devise a separate provincial plan for the internment of Vancouver's resident enemy alien poor, underscoring the province's resolve to push forward with an internment camp regardless of the schedule set out by the Internment Directorate. Within days, the province recommended creating a camp ninety miles east of the city on the main railway line, whose estimated cost was $500.

Contrary to the press reports, Ottawa was not entirely indifferent to the difficulties in Vancouver. In a quick reversal, the dominion government responded by suspending its earlier injunction preventing the departure of enemy aliens, allowing them to leave under a specially devised order-in-council (although their entry remained dependent on American approval). As for the provincial plan to create a separate internment facility near Vancouver – brusquely kiboshed by the Internment Directorate because it was seen as hastily conceived and naïve in terms of implementation – Ottawa replaced it with the original scheme to immediately create a camp in the mountain interior near Monashee, where the internees could be put to work on road construction. Also prioritized was the refurbishment of the small Vernon detention facility, which, after being hurriedly enlarged, would assume a greater role as a centre for internment in the province.

The unsettling economic conditions in British Columbia served to heighten public suspicions and resentment of the enemy alien. Allegations and hearsay were all chronicled in the major dailies, often fashioned as news. In Vancouver, a fire of unknown origin that consumed a commercial establishment was attributed to its enemy alien proprietor. When the city's Connaught and Granville bridges were damaged during a fierce windstorm, newspapers were quick to suggest that German supporters were behind the destruction.[18] These and other reports looked to keep the public apprised regarding the harm being perpetrated by enemy saboteurs, who were portrayed as shadowy figures operating in the dark.

Anti-enemy alien suspicion, however, was already at a fever pitch and was intensifying due to the distressing news from the European front. The second battle of Ypres produced enormous Canadian casualties, in part from the use of poison gas. Lists of the local dead and wounded, notably from British Columbia's 2nd Canadian Mounted Rifles, were published in the BC papers. Believing several prominent residents of German origin in Victoria had congregated to revel in the news of the German advance, neighbours called the police, insisting the members of the group be arrested and interned. Despite the protests of the gatherers, who declared that they were simply having a housewarming party, the constabulary obliged, the local press noting: "It was an unlucky time for the Germans to be celebrating anything."[19] Anger mingled freely with personal and collective grief to the point at which all reason and civility were abandoned. No quarter was to be given the enemy.

Emotions came to a boil when, a few weeks later, news was received of the torpedoing of the passenger ship *Lusitania* off the coast of Ireland, with a massive loss of civilian life. A dozen British Columbians were among the dead. On 8 May 1915, clamouring for retribution, a riotous mob in Victoria ransacked businesses identified as German-owned.[20] The anger continued the following day as a crowd demanding action gathered at BC Government House. Damage to government property was averted by troops who were stationed to protect the building. On 10 May, dreading the worst, city officials introduced martial law. In the shadow of the *Lusitania*, the BC press sought to channel the public's rage, issuing editorials calling for the boycott of German-owned businesses as well as the internment of all enemy aliens in the province.[21]

The press was unambiguous in its condemnation. Attributing the sinking of the passenger liner to German national character – "a nation of murderers" – BC papers insisted that all resident aliens of German origin renounce their native land and that those who failed to do so be exposed and rooted out as enemies: "The word German stinks in our nostrils and any man that retains the slightest connection with the German nation is beyond the pale."[22] For some readers, this proved too much, and they criticized the newspaper for fomenting ill will and inciting violence. The *Vancouver Sun* rebutted by asserting that the government was to blame. Officials were far too lenient it claimed, insisting that, when the scale of the problem was uncovered, "the people of Vancouver will realize the number of disloyal residents we have in the community."[23]

According to the press, the internment of all Germans was the only solution, including those who were naturalized. A wide net was being cast, but, as Victoria's *Daily Colonist* observed, German imperial citizenship, which applied to all Germans living abroad, made every German a natural enemy. They had to be dealt with, the paper adding: "Such action may result in inconvenience to many people who are not even remotely identified with the atrocities which the Germans have committed, but that cannot be helped.

The very name of Germany has been execrated."[24] When, after the Victoria riot, twenty-six enemy aliens in South Vancouver were corralled and sent to the Vernon internment camp – based mostly on the allegations of spiteful neighbours – this was reported as the start of Ottawa's undertaking to finally deal with the enemy alien problem. Still, the government was advised to be more resolute in its approach. According to the press, this was not the time for timidity as public patience was limited.[25]

Although Ottawa was the principal target of the press, the *Vancouver Sun,* hoping to prod the provincial government into action, launched a campaign (outlined in a series of editorials) to have all enemy aliens in British Columbia interned without exception.[26] The public embraced this initiative. The sinking of the *Lusitania* demonstrated the treachery of the enemy, which included people of enemy origin who were residing within the province. With the public's ire aroused, questions were asked: How was it that enemy aliens were going about their business undisturbed? Why were they not interned? And why were they working when patriots were without jobs? The *Vancouver Sun* queried: "Is it true that a lot of Germans are occupied in Vancouver while our own people are without work?"[27]

A seemingly innocuous question, the issue of security, nevertheless, was being linked to ordinary, everyday concerns. Unemployed enemy aliens in British Columbia had been periodically arrested, resulting in the internment of enemy-alien jobless and poor. Now, the idea of imprisoning enemy aliens *with jobs* was being contemplated to preserve employment among the native-born and Britishers. This, however, could only occur if those of foreign birth, castigated as the enemy, were dismissed from their places of work.[28] Coupling their fate with the public's appetite for retribution in the aftermath of the *Lusitania*, the push was on to expand and accelerate the process of internment by demanding the dismissal of those enemy aliens who were gainfully employed but deemed unworthy.

The issue of interning employed enemy aliens was most acute in those regions of the province and sectors of the economy where they were present in large numbers.[29] The mining camps on Vancouver Island and in the BC interior, especially in the Kootenays, were notable. In May, under public pressure, mines near Nanaimo dismissed some 115 enemy aliens. The provincial police promptly arrested and then transferred these people to the Saanich Prison Farm near Victoria, eventually moving them to the Vernon camp. Pleased with this development, the premier, William Bowser, was quoted in the press as saying that this "[was] to the advantage of white workingmen on Vancouver Island," and encouraged mine managers to hire local, non-enemy aliens as replacements. Fortified by news of these events, disgruntled native-born miners at Coal Creek and Fernie in the Crowsnest Pass staged strikes to reinforce their own calls for the discharge of enemy alien coworkers.[30] Bowser, reacting to the wishes of the disaffected strikers, instructed the province's police superintendent to intern all unmarried enemy aliens working at the mines.

The press reported that Premier Bowser, through this initiative, was effectively looking to create employment opportunities for "deserving" patriots while simultaneously eliminating a menace. The premier's action, however, was at odds with the dominion government's assurance, given at the start of the war, that enemy aliens would not be interfered with if they were law-abiding. The arrest of employed enemy aliens was illegal. For Bowser, however, this did not matter. Seeking to garner political support, he anticipated that this move would be favourably received, as indeed it was.

The *Vancouver World* welcomed the premier's decision but still looked to capitalize on the momentum by asking why a similar measure had not been extended beyond the miners to the general enemy alien population.[31] The *Vancouver Sun*, too, congratulated Bowser, praising him for his decisiveness and was critical of those politicians who were seen to be timorous in their approach. Henry Stevens, Vancouver member of Parliament, was lambasted for remarking that naturalized Canadians of German origin were not enemy aliens and therefore exempt from internment. Naturalized

Germans had to be dealt with as well, the paper argued: "Why aid and abet these inhuman monsters on the strength of ideas which were never intended for use toward mad dogs or a nation of frenzied butchers? We would like to know. The public will insist on knowing. And the sooner this spineless course ceases to be pursued the better."[32]

Under the BC premier's direction, the provincial police arrested some 317 enemy aliens in Fernie. Once taken into custody, their internment had to be addressed. Pressing his advantage, the premier petitioned the dominion government to assume responsibility for them. The request was problematic in so far as the provincial arrest of innocents undermined the basic tenets of lawful rule. Nevertheless, fearing a public backlash and unrest, Ottawa introduced Order-in-Council PC 1501, authorizing the internment of any enemy alien competing with the native-born for employment. Unprecedented in its reach, the ordinance retroactively sanctioned the arrests, pushing aside any possible legal appeals. There were some who objected to this course of action. Union leaders at the mines and Fernie's labour-supported newspaper, the *District Ledger*, tried to impress upon the colliers the importance of working-class solidarity. However, in the face of patriotic fervour, their pleas were of no avail.[33] In fact, the union leadership would lose the confidence of its members and the *District Ledger* its audience, the paper ending operations shortly after taking its unpopular and purportedly disloyal stance.

Not all who were arrested would be interned. Naturalized citizens as well as allied aliens detained in the roundup were released. Nonetheless, the numbers of those arrested were large and increasing daily as those taken within an ever wider geographic radius were brought to Fernie, where a skating rink was converted into a makeshift internment facility. This ad hoc arrangement called for more robust measures to ensure that security regulations would be met. After a leasing agreement was struck with local business interests, a hotel and its adjoining grounds were acquired at the nearby abandoned Morrissey townsite. Internment officials were persuaded that a camp at this location could be economically provisioned and the prisoners usefully put to work on local road improvements.

With PC 1501 in place, there was more latitude regarding the internment of enemy aliens, and so the number of those arrested increased. However, the new Morrissey camp and existing facilities at Vernon and Nanaimo were unable to handle the influx of internees. Consequently, internment camps were soon created elsewhere in the province. The originally proposed Monashee camp (superseded a short time later by a more accessible camp at Edgewood) was quickly organized, ensuring the continuing construction of the Monashee Mountain road. A camp at Mara Lake was created for the purpose of building a road that was to connect the towns of Enderby and Sicamous. Finally, internment camps at Revelstoke and Yoho national parks were established after similar facilities had been set up at Banff and Jasper, where enemy aliens were forced to work on improving park infrastructure.

Given the opportunity to use POW labour, the process of creating camps in British Columbia led to a mad scramble as more jurisdictions sought to secure such facilities– all of which was reported in the local press. Kelowna's mayor launched an appeal for its "fair share" of internment business and the advantages that would accrue from prisoner labour assigned to improving nearby public infrastructure. The Nelson Board of Trade petitioned for an enemy-built road between Nelson and Ymir but was turned down. After the dominion government rebuffed a similar request from the Duncan Board of Trade, board trustees pressed Duncan's parliamentary representative to take up the matter with Ottawa, reminding him that it was his duty to help with "the obstacles." Supported by the local press, they argued that there were gains to be realized and that these should not be lost. Ottawa's inclination, however, was to work with the provincial government to identify projects that would have a marked impact and be of lasting value.[34]

Sent to the BC wilderness, internees were assigned to projects that required hard, physical labour: quarrying rock, clearing forests, building fire safeguards, constructing roads. The punitive nature of the work was to be expected since they were considered enemies. Indeed, when it was discovered that some German internees at Vernon were being liberally treated, the *Vernon News* chastised the camp administration for its lax attitude: "Do the authorities responsible for the affairs of the internment camp realize this [danger]? Are they merely playing at being at war, or are they seized with the supreme gravity of the situation?"[35] The indifference of camp administrators was a matter on which the newspaper would not be silent. The "sickening deference" towards the interned enemy alien had to be replaced by an attitude that was in accord with their enemy standing.

Nor should there have been any uncertainty about the purpose of internment. Criticizing those who chafed at the expense of the operation, the *Vancouver Sun* insisted the idea that it was too costly to intern larger numbers was misguided. "Why," the editors argued, "should it be expensive? Why should not our roads be mended and some of the huge tracts of timbered land cleared for future settlers by these interned aliens? Are their hands too soft for manual labour? They should be more than self-supporting if put to work."[36] The *Sun* maintained that, if internment was an extension of war, then there could be no hesitation in dealing with enemy aliens in a way that reflected both their position in society and the nature of the conflict. According to the *Sun*, internment, and all that it entailed, was both right and appropriate because it was an expression of loyal support in the context of the empire being at war.

Not everyone agreed. According to one letter-writer, fairness was the hallmark of British civilization, and, although Germany merited punishment, the public needed to be mindful of the fact that: "Many alien enemies in Canada are the parents of natural born Canadian subjects, and but simply on the ground that they are enemy aliens, it will lead to estrangements and unhappy results when this wicked war and its horrid waste of blood and treasure will only be a memory."[37] This and other pleas for tolerance did not register; rather, they were scorned and ridiculed by the newspaper readership, which was keen on knowing that the camps were dealing appropriately with the country's enemies.

Although remoteness meant that news was scarce, in 1916, BC newspapers periodically reported on incidents at the camps, highlighting for the public not only the importance of internment but also the necessity of dealing firmly with the enemy.[38] Victoria's *Daily Colonist* noted that two prisoners assigned to the Monashee-Edgewood Road project who refused to work were bayoneted, one seriously wounded. At Morrissey, the press praised the work of sentries who fired their rifles in an effort to recapture several escaped prisoners – this was war and defiance had to be met with force. The use of force also gave some assurance to the public that internment, a military operation, was being treated with the seriousness it deserved.

Still, there was much to be concerned about. The prisoners showed themselves to be a wily and scheming lot. The *Vernon News* reported that Morrissey internees had planned an escape, and, but for the timely discovery of the plot, serious trouble could have resulted. The paper added that the plotters would not have made good their escape without help, and it surmised "that in some manner communication was established with outside parties." At the Vernon camp, the *Vancouver World* described how internees successfully tunnelled out of their enclosure, and here, too, the assistance of outside conspirators was suspected, the paper speculating that their escape could only have happened because "automobiles were awaiting them after they emerged from the tunnel."[39] These and other events pointed to the conniving nature of the internees and their confederates. The newspapers maintained that it was fortunate that internment was in place to deal with these people, whose deception and treachery knew no bounds.

Internment was used to reassure an increasingly agitated public. Yet it was important that the public's appreciation of internment's role not flag. This meant impressing upon the public the importance of pressuring Ottawa to institute a more robust form of internment, especially around the issue of employed enemy aliens. The *Vancouver Sun* declared: "If the Canadian government is to be moved in the matter, it can only be by Dominion-wide agitation and organization." Seeing this as being within the legitimate scope of press activity, the *Sun* threatened to publish the names of local businesses employing enemy aliens so that: "the people can use their own discretion as regards to dealing with Germans or the employers of Germans." The *Sun* further undertook to help organize and support the "Anti-German Union" in Vancouver to boycott German businesses as well as to unmask those politicians who would "befriend" the enemy alien.[40] In view of perceived government dallying and the missteps of business, it was crucial for the public to know that, through the application of pressure, it could bring about results. The *Sun* was adamant that diligence was needed and it was prepared to play its role, especially in view of what appeared to be a disconcerting change in government policy.

Despite the demand for more action, Ottawa demonstrated restraint, carefully weighing its options. Internment, at least initially, was used as a policy instrument to deal with enemy alien unemployment. By the end of 1916 and well into 1917, the labour situation in the country dramatically changed. Military recruitment and the needs of industry resulted in labour shortages, compelling the dominion government to revisit its policy. Companies and other business enterprises requested that Ottawa release prisoners to meet the demand for labour. In British Columbia, mining interests were especially affected by the scarcity of workers. So, in keeping with a new policy direction and at the request of business, the Internment Directorate selectively paroled prisoners to the collieries – notably those who, during their imprisonment, had been docile and acquiescent.

The change in policy was poorly received by the BC public and press. The paroled enemy alien – a former POW – was now working alongside Britishers and native-born Canadians. How was this even remotely possible? Newspapers took up the challenge. The *Daily Colonist* angrily asserted: "That [former prisoners] should receive the same wages as our own workingmen is not reasonable, nor is it reasonable that he should come into competition with our own people."[41] This fury was also directed against the provincial government, which was seen as unwilling to take a stronger stand against Ottawa's new policy course. The province was accused of complicity, its inaction interpreted as duplicitous and even unpatriotic.

Premier Bowser, especially, was reproached for colluding with mining interests at the expense of "white working men."[42] The newspapers asked: What message did reintegrating the previously interned enemy alien into the workplace convey to those whose sons and fathers had been lost on the Western Front? Was this not a betrayal? Why did business interests take precedence over the defence of the country and its interests? In letters to the editors, a few good-natured souls protested, advocating moderation. They cited blind hatred as the root of the problem and pleaded for a more charitable outlook towards their neighbours. Not to be bested, the critics responded by panning the Samaritans for their naïveté, declaring: "[Enemy aliens] would only laugh at us if we appl[ied] ordinary Christian ethical conduct to them." There could be no working alongside them, they argued, and no dealing with such "savages" for generations to come.[43]

In Nanaimo, public exasperation over the issue eventually led the municipal council there to adopt a resolution calling for the re-internment of those who had recently been released and were now working at the local colliery. Similar motions were approved and carried in Kelowna, Vernon, and other jurisdictions in the province. Mindful of the widening discontent and sensing the public would not be easily appeased, especially with the press playing a supporting role, the BC minister of mines met with Major

General William Otter, the internment director. The minister impressed upon the latter the importance of not paroling internees to industry within the province. The director, the press favourably reported, gave his assurance that "no such aliens hereafter would be given the opportunity of obtaining that form of employment, which the minister ha[d] taken objection to."[44] This, however, did not mean that prisoners would be prevented from release: they would simply be sent to other parts of the country where the need for their labour was just as great but where objection to their release not so adamant.

In view of the ongoing policy of paroling prisoners, some camps across the country would close while others were consolidated. The dominion government, believing that the BC camps had served their purpose, decommissioned them all except for Vernon and Morrissey, where several hundred internees, viewed as obstinate and untrustworthy, were kept for safekeeping. Still, Ottawa's critics thought that the ongoing discharge of prisoners was unacceptable, and this added to a long list of the government's perceived failings. Why were immigrants of enemy origin, now naturalized, allowed to have an electoral say on the politics of the country? Why were all enemy aliens in the country not interned and forced to work at POW wages? How was it that enemy aliens were allowed to earn a living wage with nary a worry while Canada's sons were being recruited to fight overseas? For Nanaimo's 'Win the War League' the problem could not have been more stark: "It is a disgrace to allow enemy aliens in Canada to grow fat at the expense of the blood of our boys in France."[45]

These concerns consumed newspaper readers who, in letters to the editor, shared their consternation at, and disbelief in, Ottawa's lax attitude. However, the dominion government resisted the demand for the wholesale internment of enemy aliens and the compulsory use of their labour, arguing that such measures would have led to nation-wide economic disruption.[46] The public was unimpressed, its anger stoked by sensational press reports regarding the alleged mistreatment of Allied soldiers in German POW camps, including prisoners being herded together with typhus victims, captive soldiers starved, officers treated as convicts, abuses culminating in shootings, and prisoners' foreheads tattooed with the German eagle.[47] These and other press stories served to inflame public passions and excoriated the enemy as being beyond redemption. Was it surprising, then, that British Columbians increasingly asked: Why had enemy aliens even been allowed entry into the country? And what was to be done with them after the war?

According to the press, a liberal immigration policy had invited these people to the country. Whether Canada would be able to attract a better class of settler was unknown. But, for the *Vancouver Sun*, only those who shared the same customs and habits were acceptable immigrants. To this end, the expulsion of the enemy alien was warranted: it was necessary to engage in a process "of weeding [them] out, instead of bringing in more."[48] It was unclear whether Ottawa understood the problem. The policy of enemy alien parole exemplified the naïveté of leadership, and it was left to patriots to compel officials to reverse course. Since Ottawa appeared indifferent to removing the enemy alien from the country, it was thought that perhaps the BC government could be convinced to do so.

Acknowledging that returning veterans in British Columbia had a singular right to voice their opinion, the press was eager to ensure their voices were heard. A proposal by the veteran's group 'League of Patriots' to have the BC government convert all mines in the province into internment camps – where every enemy alien could be put to work "at the point of bayonet" – was touted as a plan worth supporting.[49] Far more important was the idea of expelling from the province the entire enemy alien population. Since interned enemy aliens released from the BC internment camps were already being sent to other parts of the country as per the province's earlier agreement with the Internment Directorate, then why not send the entire enemy alien population? There were an estimated eighty-five hundred enemy aliens at liberty in the province. With adequate planning, this number, it was explained, could also be removed.

There was some urgency to the matter: returning veterans needed work. In Kelowna, the complaint that, at the local canneries, enemy aliens were in competition not only with veterans but also "white women" underscored the point.[50] An affront to the very foundation of British civilization, enemy aliens had to be permanently barred from British Columbia. Not everyone appeared to grasp the seriousness of the situation. Contravening the order-in-council directing that any alien competing for work be dismissed and interned, BC companies continued to employ enemy aliens. Seen as a betrayal, this treachery on the part of business had to be exposed and stopped. Thus, in Victoria, full press coverage was given to a motion before city council insisting not only that the names of firms and individuals employing enemy aliens be publicized but also that they be forced to follow the law.[51] There could be no indifference on an issue as vital as this. The enemy alien had to be removed and barred from the province, not indulged.

The stridency of the press ensured that political pressure was applied. And, although Ottawa may have been seen as unsympathetic to local needs, town councils and individual politicians could be made to follow the bidding of their constituents. Targeting municipal officials, the newspapers demanded that they, too, do more. Under the watchful eye and reporting of the press, Vancouver city council passed a resolution demanding enemy alien deportation and more stringent postwar immigration controls. The council further insisted that the BC government clear the province of the entire enemy alien population. A similar memorial supporting their expulsion was soon adopted by the city and district councils of Victoria and North Vancouver.[52] With pressure mounting, the provincial legislature passed a motion supporting the removal of all alien enemies from British Columbia.

The debate on the future of enemy aliens covered in the pages of the provincial press resonated with BC representatives in Ottawa. Not wishing to be seen as lagging on the broader question of national policy and having been the target of press criticism in the past, they soon became more vocal in the House of Commons. Member of Parliament for Burrard, S.J. Crowe, introduced a motion calling for the deportation of enemy aliens from the country. Separately, H.H. Stevens, MP for Vancouver, introduced a resolution that would have amended immigration laws, prohibiting any enemy alien from entering, let alone settling in the country. Not to be outdone by his colleagues, the parliamentarian from Comox-Alberni, H.S. Clements, advised the government to clearly define a policy that would not only expel enemy aliens from Canada but also deal with those who remained interned – especially given the signing of the recent armistice. Their continuing internment after the armistice was sufficient proof that they needed to be expelled – and immediately. The enemy alien prisoner, the press reported Clements as saying, was "just as much an enemy today as he was during the war, and he should be deported at the earliest opportunity. The authorities should not wait for palatial ships to take them from Canada: cattle ships were good enough."[53]

With the armistice, the seeming procrastination and indecision of governments regarding the question of expulsion resulted in growing frustration among veterans. Despite statements of support, there appeared to be no follow through. When local veterans in Kelowna discovered that the city council had approved but then filed away a submission calling for the deportation of enemy aliens, they threatened violence, thus forcing the councillors to reconsider.[54] In Calgary and Winnipeg, veterans were less understanding: rioting occurred after their petitions were ignored. Suggesting that similar disturbances could take place in British Columbia, the *Daily Colonist* argued that the provincial government needed "to bring forcibly to the attention of the [dominion] Government the attitude of the Province on the subject [of deportation]."[55] The

Vancouver Sun was adamant that the anger of the veterans in Calgary and Winnipeg had been triggered by the ongoing employment of enemy aliens in those cities and, more deeply still, by government prevarication on the issue.[56] The newspaper warned that, unless Ottawa acted to rid the country of both enemy aliens and the agitators who roused them, the situation in Vancouver could turn ugly as well. The *Sun* added that, if the dominion government was "waiting for public opinion to get behind them and urge them along, [then] the process of making up their minds [would] be aided by the knowledge that the attitude of this province [was] emphatic ... It [was] not a problem of statesmanship. No particular ability [was] required to tell these people to get out and stay out."[57]

Ottawa was aware of the seriousness of the situation. The growing postwar labour unrest in western Canada rattled officials. Sensing trouble, the situation forced dominion officials to take proactive steps. Believing at the very least that there was merit in deporting those still behind barbed wire, the government, under pressure, initiated the enumeration of prisoners in the remaining internment camps – Vernon among them – who, in the estimation of the commanding officers, could not be trusted. To this group were added labour-political activists and protestors who had been recently arrested during the growing labour unrest in the country and were interned under the war powers of the government, which were still in effect.[58] It was only a matter of time before scheduled arrangements regarding their deportation were finalized.

In late February 1919, at the Vernon camp, where 353 enemy aliens were interned, one hundred were chosen for deportation and sent east in preparation for transport overseas. With unrest brewing in Winnipeg, the removal of the remaining prisoners was expedited. On 2 June 1919, an additional 163 Vernon prisoners were assembled for deportation, leaving some ninety in the camp. Among those selected were thirty-three children and twenty-two women, the latter whom the internment director considered "as a rule to be even more disloyal than their husbands." The camp at Vernon continued to operate until February 1920 – viewed as a necessity since, as the press noted, the RNWMP commissioner was convinced that many "troublesome aliens would still have to be interned in western Canada."

The deportation of interned enemy aliens was one of the last acts pertaining to the Great War in Canada. The immigration question, however, remained unresolved. Calls for a more rigorous immigration policy persisted throughout 1919 and beyond. Labour troubles were proof positive of the need for greater controls on immigration to ensure that only desirable migrants would be allowed to enter and settle in Canada. In the opinion of the press, certain immigrants could never be assimilated: "As a silk purse cannot be made from a pig's ear so it is also impossible to develop a fine nationhood with human riffraff for material."

Advocating for quality not quantity, the press put legislators on notice that there was "no excuse for failing to give Canada an immigration policy which [would] produce citizens, not parasites."[59] In British Columbia, the demand was not only to bar former enemies from entering Canada but also Asians, Indians, Hutterites, and Dukhobors. As for those enemy aliens from other provinces who were now naturalized and wished to settle in British Columbia, they were unwelcome. Made aware that a group from Saskatchewan was prepared to disembark from a boat on Lake Okanagan, a hostile veteran-led crowd turned them away at the lakeside wharf, vowing there would be no alien colony in Kelowna.[60]

Despite the opposition and nativist rhetoric, immigrant labour was still needed. The focus of the conversation, therefore, slowly shifted from an outright ban on foreign immigration from non-British regions of the globe to restrictions. The government championed a literacy test, which would allow into the country only those who could read and write English. But here, too, the editors of the *Vancouver Sun* discerned a problem. A clause that insisted on literacy could very well "prevent some good upstanding Englishman, Scotchman, or Irishman from coming into Canada, the only objection to him being that he could not read," while "some immigrants who came to Canada read and wrote too much and did not want to do anything else."[61]

A more fitting bar, it was argued, would be to extend by several years the time allowed between the point of settlement and the granting of a certificate of naturalization. Roundly supported by the press, this measure would enable authorities to gauge whether or not the applicant was worthy of being a Canadian citizen. As for those of questionable character, newspapers wildly embraced the passage of a bill revoking naturalization certificates, arguing that the standards of civilization might yet be maintained, even on the frontier, by limiting the undesirable and removing those who did not belong.

Many immigrants originating from enemy lands were invited to Canada to labour in the factories, forests, and fields. They were accepted in so far as they followed the laws, obeyed authority, and respected public order. Yet, acceptance was also a function of war's progress (or lack thereof). Consequently, many issues were filtered through this lens. Of prime concern was loyalty. At a time of war, could those that Canada invited to its shores be trusted? An open question, it nevertheless belied notions already fixed in imperial ideas and beliefs. Disloyalty was suspected by those who felt that birthright and loyalty were inseparable, and this had enormous consequences. Immigrants who had originated from belligerent lands, and whose allegiance was therefore in doubt, were presumed enemies. It was believed by many that they did not belong – a view inherent within the larger narrative of global and civilizational struggle.

Distressing overseas news and lists of local casualties published in the BC press translated effortlessly into a belief in the barbarism of the enemy. With enemy aliens being ubiquitous, it was imperative that patriots be made aware of the danger. And because so much was at stake, the rhetoric became ever more censorious and virulent in tone. Nothing and no one was spared. BC newspapers depicted Germany as "a nation of murderers," while resident enemy aliens were seen as likely conspirators. With security being the focus, this perceived threat became immediate and real, bringing attention to the notion that aliens of enemy origin were never meant to be in Canada.

In British Columbia, it was unclear whether the dominion government understood this, accounting for the public's disappointment with Ottawa's seeming indifference regarding either the role that expanded internment might play or the idea of expelling enemy aliens from the country. However, the dominion government, in an abundance of caution, was careful to manage the problem in keeping with its own priorities and assessment. So, it was left to the public, encouraged by the BC press, to insist that the government do more. The goal of the press and public was to impress upon the government the importance of decision and resolve. Enemy aliens were more than a problem: they were a threat. And so the discourse around the enemy alien was shaped by pressure to which officials at different government levels were expected to respond.

In British Columbia, several initiatives were roundly supported by a public eager to see that enemy aliens were being properly handled: the creation of an independent provincial agency to oversee arrests – the so-called Department of Alien Reservists; the province's internment of enemy aliens who were competing with the native-born for jobs (retroactively approved by Ottawa); the purging of all those in internment camps from the province; and, indeed, the expulsion of the entire enemy alien population. The zeal with which these initiatives were championed signalled the uncompromising opposition of a populace already accustomed to think of the foreigner in civilizational and racialized terms – "white" versus "non-white," "cultured" versus "uncultured," "deserving" versus "undeserving" – and who were keen on an even more robust postwar immigration policy. There was no place for the enemy in Canada, and any contribution to ensuring the realization of this goal was welcome.

Throughout, the press encouraged and shaped opinion in British Columbia. Occasionally, its criticism of the enemy alien would be overt, editorializing, for example, on the importance of internment as a mechanism not only for control but also for removal. More subtly, however, it looked to highlight the shortcomings of internment administrators and the unwise practices of governments while praising and cajoling those politicians who could be influenced. In these and other respects, the press conditioned the public to be harsh in its judgment of enemy aliens, always emphasizing the nature of the threat they posed and what needed to be done about it: "It remains for the people of Canada to say whether or not they wish further to expose the lives of women and children to these fiends in human form. The *Sun* is not seeking to take credit for the agitation which has swept [Vancouver] during the past week. We feel simply that it is a matter of duty which every man in this city and in this country should perform."[62]

There were compelling reasons for the public to follow the press and accept its crusading rhetoric. To be sure, danger of any sort could not be ignored, increasing the public's appreciation for vigilance, but it was also the case that patriotism lent the anti-enemy alien discourse an air of authenticity. There was, in effect, no reason to distrust the press, if only because the majority of the province's population was already inclined to think in terms of empire and civilization, as evidenced by the countless letters to the editor in the various dailies. The ideology of imperialism framed the question of belonging and, in the context of war, helped identify the enemy and the risk they represented. All that remained was for the government to do more and, to this end, public feeling was mobilized to pressure officials who were expected to do their duty.

In its role of mobilizing public opinion, the press demonstrated little restraint. Indeed, throughout the conflict, and in different ways – reporting, for instance, on the purported treachery and deceit of the enemy alien – the press continuously catechized its readers, asking: What kind of country do you want? This question resonated with many who believed that Canada should stand firmly with the motherland – an imperial idea that guided people who believed that doing so would serve the nation well into the future. However, there was a more menacing current of opinion that framed the question of the country's future – Canada had to be rid of those who had no business being here, a view that, with few exceptions, the BC press encouraged.

5

A Mountain Requiem

Internment in Canada's Rocky Mountains National Park, 1915–17

On 15 February 1916, W.J. Roche, Canada's minister of the interior, rose in Parliament to address a question posed by opposition member Frank Oliver regarding whether it was the intention of the government to use labour from one of the internment camps recently established in Canada's mountain parks. The minister replied that interned enemy aliens would be put to work in accordance with military schedules and paid twenty-five cents per day – the wage allotted war prisoners. Having them sit idle – "eating their heads off" – would not be countenanced, he said.[1] When pressed about their work conditions and what they would do, Roche stated that, under military guard, the prisoners would build roads, clear brush, and generally clean up the national park. He further stipulated that their labour would not be voluntary because only in this way could it be ensured that a lot of work would get done.

Oliver reproached the minister, arguing that the compulsory labour of those interned by the government was a very serious problem. As recent immigrants without jobs, it was unimaginable that they would be used this way. "These people," Oliver claimed, "have not committed any crime against the laws of the country, and, while I can appreciate the desirability of interning them and offering them the opportunity of employment, when it comes down to compulsory employment at twenty-five cents a day, I am afraid that this involves principles which we cannot all subscribe to."[2] For Oliver, these were civilians who happened to be interned. The forcible use of their labour in the parks, he insisted, was unprincipled. Roche, however, was unmoved. By equating their situation to that faced by captured British soldiers, and by paying them a POW wage, Roche made it clear that they were war prisoners in every sense of the term and that, as such, there was nothing untoward about using them in this way. Moreover, believing that Germany's dreadful treatment of British POWs would offset any criticism, he did not expect international repercussions. Enemy aliens who were interned in Canada would be put to work.

The exchange between Roche and Oliver appeared to highlight differences in understanding regarding the status of interned enemy aliens. For Roche, internees were war prisoners, and they were to be treated as such. Oliver, on the other hand, considered them civilians and therefore deserving of consideration. This contrast pointed to the ambiguity in their legal status. Still, for both Roche and Oliver, internment helped to address the problem of enemy alien joblessness. Their disagreement, therefore, was one of degree, not of kind.

Yet, for Oliver, the question of how exactly these people were to be treated while interned – a function of their ambiguous status – was a contested one.[3] Could the internees be compelled to work? According to the opposition member of Parliament, their civilian status suggested that they could not. So, what does the internment experience tell us about how this discrepancy was overcome, and what were the implications of this? No less important, how was internment understood not only by the wider public but also by those in charge and the internees themselves? And how could the goal of developing Canada's parks as a symbol of national pride be reconciled with the idea of forcibly putting civilians to work as war prisoners?

These were pressing questions, offering insight into the nature of internment at camps located in Banff and nearby Castle Mountain where, between 1915 and 1917, immigrants of enemy origin were sent to labour in Canada's Rocky Mountains National Park. Against a backdrop of ambition and indifference, unfortunates – innocent civilians – would be forced to work under military guard. As a result, an astonishing tale of brutality, humiliation, survival, and perseverance would unfold, and although the experience mirrored similar developments at other internment stations on Canada's frontiers, it remains very much a story of the making of Canada's premier national park. It is a story that brings attention to the contradiction faced by those who were initially invited to the country and then rejected, of civilians who would be treated as war prisoners although having nothing to do with the war. It is a story that echoed in the incongruity of a setting celebrated for its splendour and restorative powers but that had become a place of darkness and anguish. Jarring in its details, this is a tale as unimaginable as it was real, becoming one of the more remarkable and improbable stories of Banff National Park.

With the advent of the First World War, immigrants originating from enemy lands became targets of nativist hostility in Canada, a problem exacerbated by their lack of fit within an ailing economy rapidly shifting towards war. Dismissed from places of work, their rates of unemployment soared. To deal with the problem, public attention was naturally drawn to the utility of employing emergency powers under the War Measures Act. These included expanding the practice of internment, introduced for security reasons during the war's opening stages but, until this point, having had limited use.[4] Order-in-Council PC 2721, issued under the WMA, stated unequivocally that aliens of enemy birth who were without employment or means would be interned and put to work as war prisoners.

In the months to follow, rising joblessness and privation among enemy aliens led to the detention of hundreds in military prisons and, as the numbers grew, in hastily organized holding facilities. Under pressure, the newly created Internment Directorate scrambled to secure more permanent accommodations. In eastern Canada negotiations with the military and the provincial governments of Ontario and Quebec led to the creation of internment camps at Petawawa and Valcartier and then Kapuskasing and Spirit Lake. The large number of enemy aliens detained in holding stations at Winnipeg, Brandon, Lethbridge, and Nanaimo spurred a similar search for partners in Canada's west. Early on, the idea of using POWs to develop Canada's national parks was bandied about. However, it was not until the use of internment labour was authorized under PC 2721 that F.H. Williamson, the deputy commissioner of the Parks Branch, sensing an opportunity, wrote a memo touting the benefits that would accrue from the use of prisoners for parks development.[5] Williamson argued that locating internment camps in the national parks could address the problem of how to hold POWs securely. In the wilderness, he explained, escape was impossible.

The focus on security was strategic on Williamson's part. So, too, was the argument that the work would provide employment relief for the many jobless enemy aliens.[6] However, what mattered most for branch officials was the development of the parks, an enterprise in which internment labour could play a role. In the context of austerity budgets – the Rocky Mountains National Park (Banff) faced a two-thirds budget reduction and the national parks system a 50 per cent financial cut – internment presented an opportunity.[7] Williamson laid out the goals and rationale for internment in Canada's national parks. Tapping into this pool of labour, interned enemy aliens would work for the parks under the watchful eye of the military. With nowhere to flee, the idle hands of the enemy alien would be put to productive use.

Williamson's memo was sent to the Department of Justice, under whose authority the newly organized Internment Directorate fell, and then on to the Department of Militia and Defence, which was tasked with overseeing the operations. The newly appointed director of internment, Brigadier General (later Major General) William Otter, received the proposal favourably, persuaded as he was by the security that wilderness isolation could provide. There was also the opportunity to work with partners, given the fiscal limitations under which the military operation was placed. On a fact-finding mission to western Canada, Otter arranged to meet with the park commissioner, J.B. Harkin, at the Banff railway depot on 12 March 1915. Given their mutual interests and the advantages that could be obtained through cooperation, an agreement in principle was struck.

Still, the proposal had to be politically approved. Hoping for back-channel support, Harkin met with ranking political figures from the province of Alberta, Senator James Lougheed and R.B. Bennett, member of Parliament for Calgary, and impressed upon them the value of the plan. Lougheed was sympathetic to the proposal. So, too, was Bennett, whose electoral riding included the Rocky Mountains National Park. Bennett, however, would lend his support only if there were assurances that the prisoners would be employed in remote regions of the park, where they would not encounter the local population. He further insisted they were not to be coddled. It would have been "monstrous," Bennett tendered, if enemy aliens were better treated than "our own people."[8] That the proposal had civilians deployed as POWs did not warrant comment, underscoring the priority assigned to getting the enemy alien poor off the streets and out of view. With necessary political support in hand, Harkin persuaded the interior minister of the plan's feasibility and benefits; interned because they were without jobs, they at least now could be put to good use. In early June 1915, it was announced that enemy alien internees would be sent to the parks to work as war prisoners.

Some three miles west of Castle, Alberta, a junction on the Canadian Pacific Railway line, lay the terminal point of the still unfinished Banff–Lake Louise motorway. Part of a long-term strategy to increase tourism to the area, the idea was to extend the road from Castle Mountain to Lake Louise (Laggan) and then, crossing the continental divide, on to Field, British Columbia. After some initial difficulties, a site was selected and prepared at the foot of Castle Mountain in the early days of July. An enclosure – 120 by 240 feet – was erected, consisting of ten-foot posts that supported twenty horizontal strands of barbed wire spaced six inches apart. Canvas tents for the troops and enemy alien internees were also set up. Scheduled to hold two hundred prisoners, the encampment could accommodate four hundred – the total expected given the anticipated arrest of large numbers of enemy aliens in nearby Calgary. Meanwhile, the provisioning of the camp was contracted out to local Banff businesses, which were "expected to benefit very much, financially, by the arrangement."[9]

With these preliminaries attended to, the first contingent of sixty prisoners arrived from the internment facility at Lethbridge on 15 July 1915. More followed within days, for a total of 191. All were of Austro-Hungarian origin – Ukrainians, Poles, Croats, and others – and mostly common labourers. Prisoners of German nationality remained at Lethbridge, which was set aside for so-called "first-class" POWs, effectively distinguishing the internment camps, at least initially, based on class and ethnicity. Those newly arrived were put to work immediately, clearing trees and removing dead and fallen timber not only from the route of the road but also within a hundred feet to either side of the proposed throughway. The remainder were assigned to cut trees within three to four hundred feet of the nearby railway line to give the valley an open, park like appearance, thus providing train passengers with unobstructed sightlines.[10] Harvested timber was to be set aside for government use on a variety of public projects.[11]

Except for Sundays, the prisoners followed a routine of intense physical labour. Considered "second-class" POWs (as opposed to "officer class"), they were expected to work steadily.[12] Save for a thirty-minute repast, the prisoners laboured ten hours a day without rest, not including the time spent walking to and from the worksite. Declaring the internees "enemies of our country," the local Banff newspaper, the *Crag and Canyon*, insisted that those guarding the prisoners needed to be mindful of this fact, ensuring that the prisoners worked hard and long hours.[13] There was no place for them in the country, the paper asserted, and the only way they would understand this was to have them feel the bitter sting of labour.

The regular and constant arrival of arrested enemy aliens placed logistical pressure on the camp's operations. Nonetheless, those immediately responsible expressed their satisfaction and welcomed even more prisoners, citing the importance of the work – a perspective that resonated with a public that saw their labour as "good business for the Government."[14] Yet the work was of benefit only if costs were kept to a minimum. Agreeing to cover the POW labour allowance, the Parks Branch demanded value for money. Schedules and quotas, therefore, had to be closely monitored. But the Internment Directorate also shared in the costs, and it, too, looked to keep expenditures to a minimum. This demanded scrupulous oversight in provisioning the camp. The consequences of the twin imperatives of efficiency and austerity soon became apparent.

With conditions being unremitting, escapes soon became commonplace. When several prisoners were caught with wire cutters and hammers in their possession in preparation for their getaway, the *Crag and Canyon* commented: "There must be a screw loose somewhere in the present system of the camp."[15] When eight managed to flee in the days to follow, the paper repeated its assertion that all was not right. The escape of the odd individual was not the problem, the editors argued – the alarming prospect of four or five hundred desperate men marauding about the country was.

There was ample reason for this unacceptable situation. To carry out basic duties, a camp of four hundred prisoners required an estimated 140 soldiers. The existing complement of 113, which included officers, was insufficient. Twelve-hour shifts of continuous sentry duty combined with other duties was the norm. With a shortage of personnel and little respite from the demanding routine, fatigue and inattentiveness frequently set in, fostering prisoner daring.

Several escapes occurred during August and September, raising concerns about the camp's administration. When five internees fled all at once on 18 October, the commandant, Major Duncan Stuart, was forced to explain. The sentries, he claimed, were overworked, while the cutback in rations – following instructions from the Internment Directorate to reduce costs – resulted in fatigue among the troops. Nonetheless, the commandant assured headquarters that adjustments would be made to prevent further escapes, which by this time numbered twenty-eight. When another five inmates fled three weeks later, the commanding officer admitted that the problem was more deep-seated. The prisoners risked escape, Stuart argued, because of the inclement mountain weather and lack of adequate attire. He had appealed to headquarters for suitable clothing on ten different occasions but was ignored. In the meantime, the situation had become untenable. "During October," Stuart wrote, "the prisoners complained bitterly of want of boots and overalls and having to sleep without fires; one prisoner who escaped left a letter to a friend saying he preferred to take the chance of being shot escaping rather than live under the conditions."[16]

The internees' letters confirmed that the situation at Castle was dreadful and worsening. Dmytro Tkachyk wrote that, to compel them to work, ailing prisoners were shackled and placed in a dark cell on a punishment diet of bread and water for long stretches of time.[17] Nick Olinyk spoke of his ordeal in a censored letter to his wife: "As you know there are men running away from here every day because the conditions are very poor, so that we cannot go on much longer. We are not getting enough to eat. We are hungry as dogs. They are sending us to work, as they don't believe us. We are very weak."[18] That Olinyk and others were faint from hunger was unsurprising. The number of calories in a standard internment ration was 2,596, while the estimated energy required for a man at work was 2,903. This shortfall was the consequence of a cut in expenses and the introduction of food substitutes. The cost per meal had decreased from an initial twelve and a half cents to five and one-fifth cents, while meat was replaced with rice or rolled oats, fermented cabbage substituted for vegetables, and unleavened flour for bread.[19]

The number of escapes at Castle Mountain concerned General Otter, but he believed a change in venue would improve the situation. The approach of winter in the mountains made relocation necessary, and the mineral hot springs at the Cave and Basin, with its bathing pavilion and bunkhouses, was ideal. Major Stuart concurred, believing that relocating to Banff would help enormously. Following preparations for closing the Castle camp, the inmates were marched the thirty-five kilometres down the road to Banff on 9 November 1915. It was reported that, while in Banff, the prisoners would to be put to work on several municipal and park improvement projects.

Despite the move to Banff and the new quarters, the difficulties did not abate. The American consular representative in Calgary, Samuel Reat – a neutral diplomatic observer – received a smuggled letter from the camp in which internees complained about both their treatment and camp conditions, pleading for him to investigate. The consul arrived at the camp and, during inspection, took note of a range of shortcomings: overcrowding, dimly lit quarters, deficient mattresses (the paillasses, normally packed with straw, were left empty), worn footwear, and a lack of gloves, socks, and underwear. Additionally, he chronicled abuses and intimidation at the camp. Sergeant Little freely admitted to firing his rifle at J. Hawrysynyzn but stated that his intention was only to frighten the prisoner, not shoot him. Prisoner C. Bota reported sick at the infirmary and, instead of examining him, the medical sergeant, pointing a revolver, instructed him to get back to work. Similarly, prisoner A. Chiskolok, claiming illness, was forced back to work after "the guard struck him with a rifle butt and called him a son-of-a-bitch."[20]

Presented with Reat's report, Otter commented that, although the behaviour was unfortunate, it was not uncommon. Similar incidents, he explained, took place at other camps. However, the officer commanding Military District No. 13 (Alberta), Brigadier General E. Cruickshank, was less philosophical as the issue of excessive force had previously been taken up with the camp's commandant. In a memo to Major Stuart, Cruickshank instructed that the prisoners had to be treated with greater care: "In this connection [I] invite your attention to Chapter 14 of the Army Act as laid down in the Manual of Military Law, in which the laws and customs for the treatment of Prisoners of War are laid down ... inhumanity must not be exercised by guards over Prisoners of War."[21] Cruickshank considered the internees to be POWs and entitled to fair treatment under the laws of war. Still, for the general contractors overseeing the work of the prisoners, this was problematic: without force and intimidation, how would the work ever get done?

The reports of abuses were disquieting. However, it was the growing number of other problems at the camp that convinced Major General Otter steps needed to be taken. Inebriated guards had discharged their rifles on the streets of Banff; two soldiers were discovered intoxicated while on duty; and another purportedly gave alcohol to a prisoner work gang. All were found guilty and disciplined. The measures, however, did not appear to register with the detachment. Not long thereafter, in a drunken state, two senior non-commissioned officers demolished the camp orderly room and blamed the damage on a fictitious intruder of Chinese origin. An inquiry was also conducted regarding a private who purportedly gave a prisoner money in exchange for favours. This was all too much for the internment director. Feeling compelled to visit the Banff camp in late November, Otter, after an inspection, asked for Major Stuart's resignation.

By Otter's estimation, the situation at the camp was out of hand. The turmoil, however, was not difficult to understand. The fiery destruction of the Parliament buildings in Ottawa fed rumours of sabotage, and over two days in early February 1916, soldiers of the Canadian Expeditionary Force recruitment battalions in nearby Calgary rioted, destroying establishments identified as German-owned.[22] Isolated and powerless, the Banff detachment's unhappy fate was to watch over enemy civilians. Such responsibilities had been neither contemplated nor imagined by the detail. Many were bitter at having been unable to get overseas, where the real fight was taking place. Indeed, when a recruiting officer came calling, a full quarter of the men eagerly sought transfers. Such an exodus, however, would have undermined the security of the camp, and the guards, denied and resentful, directed their frustrations at the prisoners. Still, this did not prevent Private George Lomax, whose application had been declined, from boldly and directly making plain his wish in a letter to the military district commander that he be "liberated from this place."[23]

Although every precaution was taken, the internees kept fleeing in large numbers. After escapes took place in January and February, a proposal was made to reduce the ratio of prisoners to guards. But this meant fewer prisoners at work, and, from the perspective of park officials, their labour was much too valuable. The idea, consequently, was rejected in favour of increasing the number of troops. The addition of ten extra soldiers made no difference. Several weeks later, three prisoners escaped, followed by another, and then two more who fled under a withering volley of gunfire. The risk of being shot failed to serve as a deterrent. Indeed, a few weeks later, seven more prisoners broke free from two separate work gangs on the road project along the Spray River, again under gunfire. The guards' poor marksmanship convinced the new commandant, Major Peter Spence, that the detachment required further training. From that point on, a routine of shooting competitions was introduced to help improve the troopers' aim.

Of the fugitives from the Spray River Road project, several were recaptured despite assistance from colliers working at the nearby coal mine, who, being ethnic kindred, gave them provisions and directions. The *Crag and Canyon* reported that, having been found out, these "good Samaritans" were arrested and sent to the Banff camp to supplement the "menagerie" there.[24] Aiding and abetting the enemy was not without risk, and the consequences were well known. Yet, for the colliers – who themselves were confronted daily with the prospect of arrest and internment – the fugitives' predicament resonated. There could be no turning away. Indeed, they understood well the arbitrariness of state-sanctioned measures as these applied to enemy aliens – a point made abundantly clear in the case of John Kondro, who, without papers, was arrested and interned at Banff/Castle Mountain. Although Jacob Kondro, the father, claimed that his seventeen-year-old son was a Canadian citizen, his petition for the boy's release was ignored.[25] Suspicion and disdain were enough to keep young Kondro behind barbed wire. An enemy he would remain.

The purpose of internment was to have the prisoners work, and work they did on a variety of projects. A large contingent was assigned to a rock crusher at the foot of the western face of Mount Rundle, preparing gravel for road construction. Others cut trees and cleared bush for the new St Julian housing subdivision in Banff. Several gangs laboured on building a bridge on the Spray River and constructed a steep carriage road through the Sundance Canyon up to the Upper Hot Springs. Fencing the buffalo paddock near the Cascade River east of Banff and clearing it for pasture was also authorized work, as was filling in a depression, prone to flooding, around the grand Frank Lloyd Wright pavilion at the centre of the town's Recreation Park. Near the pavilion, prisoners built three tennis courts while another group was assigned to repair pavement on Banff's main street.[26]

The impressive number of projects was cited in diplomatic correspondence. But so, too, was the way they were completed, which elicited diplomatic protest. Receiving information that German civilians were now among the prisoners forced to work, Berlin determined that the situation at Banff was unacceptable.[27] Given the gravity of the matter, Berlin requested that the new US consul in Calgary, Harold Clum, conduct a visit to Banff in May 1916 and provide a detailed report on conditions there. The consul, revealing his prejudices, relayed that there had been nothing remiss in their treatment. As immigrant workers, they were already habituated to the work.[28] Presented with Clum's report and acknowledging that the regime of compulsory labour was problematic, officials in the British Foreign Office guilefully argued that, since the prisoners appeared not to complain, it was best if nothing were said.[29] In the wilderness and far from view, would anyone care, let alone know?

If evidence of wrongdoing was ignored and hidden, the sheer number of escapes made plain the distressing reality of the camp. Totalling sixty-one by June 1916, the figure highlighted the extent to which internees were willing to take risks. Deeply worried, Major General Otter wrote the Banff commander, Major Spence, that stronger measures needed to be introduced to staunch the exodus.[30] Otter, however, was acutely aware of the constraints under which the operation was conducted, making robust adjustments unlikely. His plan, for example, to divide the Banff camp into two smaller stations – with the aim of making each more manageable – was opposed by Park Commissioner J.B. Harkin.[31] Dividing the camp would have unnecessarily complicated and even jeopardized construction of the road to Lake Louise, a valuable project that depended on the return of all the prisoners to the Castle Mountain site. The entire group, Harkin insisted, had to remain intact to ensure that as much work as possible could get done during the coming season. Since the Parks Branch paid the POW allowance, Harkin's wishes could not be ignored.

Although disappointed, the internment director was not entirely opposed to bringing the prisoners back to the Castle site. The change of venue, Otter felt, might lighten the mood at the camp. He was also persuaded that, by concentrating the prisoners on the one job, they at least might be more easily handled. Before this could take place, however, the internees, still in Banff, were put to work on finishing, as much as possible, the road to the Upper Hot Springs and building an access route to the Banff Springs Hotel golf course. A satellite crew was also sent to repair the wharf at nearby Lake Minnewanka and renew the grounds around the hamlet to increase its allure as a tourist destination. By June's end, the internees, 312 in total, were gathered up and returned to Castle Mountain.

Upon arrival, the men picked up where they had left off the season before. Road construction had yielded substantial results: 12.8 acres were cleared, 14.7 acres grubbed of tree roots, 11,243 cubic feet of earth excavated, 380 cubic feet of loose and solid rock removed, and 10,600 linear feet of logs prepared – all by hand.[32] Progress for the next four months would be no less appreciable.[33] Out of the thick mountain forest the prisoners carved four miles of road, with 15,700 cubic feet of earth removed. A major permanent bridge consisting of iron beams and concrete abutments was also constructed over Baker Creek. Work on the project was facilitated by the addition of a steam shovel, which proved enormously useful since 136 internees had been released to industry at the end of July, replacing native-born workers who enlisted to join the fight in Europe.

The reduction in the number of enemy aliens held at internment camps across the country led to the closure of several stations, including Brandon on 30 July 1916, from which a final 103 prisoners were transferred to Castle, bringing its total back up to 279. The closure of certain camps and the consolidation of the rest signalled the beginning of a shift in the government's internment policy. In helping to rid municipalities of impoverished, jobless enemy aliens, the policy of internment had delivered. Now with improvement in the economy and demand for labour high, internment, as it was being conducted, became increasingly problematic. Nevertheless, the initial idea that it was a security measure still held in so far as some prisoners demonstrated opposition to their imprisonment and were therefore considered a risk. Thus, despite the arrival at the camp of company representatives hoping to procure labour for the Canadian Pacific Railway, the Canada Cement Company, and local collieries, the business of keeping watch remained; so, too, did the business of developing the infrastructure of the park.

The misery that accompanied internment was especially unsettling in the context of the scheme to use civilian POW labour to develop Canada's parks. Harkin, the park commissioner, a longtime proponent of the healing power of nature, wrote that, during the turmoil of war, Canada's national parks could serve as a balm to help salve the nation's wounds. Places of rest, contemplation, and recreation, the parks had the potential to still angry hearts and repair spirits broken by war. Since caring for the country's citizens was as important as defeating the enemy, support for the development of the parks, in his view, was an expression of patriotic duty. Harkin admitted, however, without a jot of irony or guilt, that the goal was being achieved, in part, through the work of those brought to the parks as forced labour.[34]

The contradiction between the redemptive power of the parks and the perfunctory assignment of civilians as compulsory labour was striking and could only be resolved if such individuals were viewed as existing outside the community. That they were vagrant immigrants helped frame this perspective. In the context of war, however, the meaning of this was made more explicit, especially where other priorities, such as park development, arose. Not only were interned enemy aliens to be put to work but, if necessary, they were to be compelled. As a result, their situation could be overlooked and even ignored.

Nowhere was this more apparent than in the indifference of the visitors who called at the camp. Newspaper reporters, day trekkers, even the Duke and Duchess of Connaught (the governor general and his spouse) all made their way to the site and, invited to stay the night, spent time marvelling at the majestic mountains all about them. Come morning, they were treated to hot buttered toast and coffee or even a hearty breakfast. Some were clearly moved and shared their impressions in the local paper, proclaiming, as one correspondent did, that "the fresh, cool air of the morning makes one think that this old world is a mighty pleasant place to live in."[35] But such assessments were possible only if the hundreds of internees in the adjoining compound were conveniently ignored. The belief that this was the fate of the enemy hardly needed stating and, indeed, was not. Yet they were civilians. So why was it that they were here? The contrast between the serene landscapes and the sight of inmates listlessly shuffling to and fro behind barbed wire made the question even more pressing. Because enemy prisoners did not matter, such contrasts went unnoticed.

For the internees, on the other hand, the juxtaposition between their own confinement and the beckoning expanse of the mountains was all too surreal. A few succumbed to mental anguish. On several occasions, Mike Penziwater slipped silently away from his work assignment only to return voluntarily in a state of confusion after spending nights alone in the deep forest. He made his final getaway attempt under a hail of bullets – five shots, all missing their mark. Upon returning, he wandered about the camp in a state of agitation, whereupon it was recommended that he be sent to the provincial asylum along with several other inmates who also demonstrated signs of instability. No action was taken, however. Only when Penziwater attacked another prisoner in a fit of uncontrolled rage was he charged with being clinically delusional and carted away.[36]

Internment was not easily borne, and Penziwater was but one of those who suffered psychologically from captivity – a duress felt all the more deeply for its basic injustice. Indeed, most internees felt aggrieved, believing they were not meant to be in a camp for POWs. Anxious about the future, rumour and speculation fuelled their fears. What was to become of them and their families? Uncertainty would take its toll, though many clung stubbornly to the belief that they were innocent. To the persistent question of what they had done to deserve this fate there was no reply because it was judged that none was needed.

The experience of internment cast a long shadow and was felt in more ways than one. Wasyl Perchaliuk was paroled from the Castle camp, with twenty-five others, to the Canmore Coal Company.[37] Suffering from a debilitating respiratory ailment, he was unable to fulfill the terms of his parole with the mine, at which point, in late November 1916, he enlisted as a private with the 211th Overseas Infantry Battalion. Poised for deployment, Perchaliuk was recognized by a former Castle camp officer as an internee. Removed from the ranks for questioning, the recruit admitted he had been a prisoner at the camp. Being in violation of the order-in-council prohibiting enemy aliens from enlisting, he was held at the Calgary military detention cells. His return to Castle as a war prisoner was a foregone conclusion. Ashamed and made despondent by the prospect of being interned once again, Perchaliuk, alone in a cell and still in uniform, committed suicide.

There was no hiding from one's plight as an enemy alien, either inside or outside the camp. It was an unenviable position, and for those imprisoned what the future might hold was a matter of chance. Release could occur at any time. Indeed, between late

August and mid-November 1916, eighty-seven internees were discharged to industry, giving rise to the question: Why risk escape and tempt fate when parole was a possibility? After POW No. 290, Petro Konowalczuk, was shot twice in the back and abdomen while attempting to flee, it made sense simply to bide one's time.[38] Still, being either unable or unwilling to live with uncertainty, a few took a chance at flight. Two leapt from the local train during transport, only to be recaptured. Another used wire cutters to slip through the compound fence at night, while a prisoner-cook from the field kitchen detail seized the opportunity to flee under the cover of smoke and disappeared forever.

These escapes were indicative of the ongoing desperate situation at Castle camp. Threadbare clothing was a source of constant complaint, as was a lack of boots, socks, and mitts. Scarcity of food was also a problem. In protest, some internees damaged their shovels, resulting in punishment diets (bread and water) and solitary confinement. As for the guards, who became increasingly irascible, a variety of provocations and misconduct took place, including a soldier shooting another in the leg. Disciplinary action was meted out for the most severe offences. This sometimes went beyond what Canadian Army regulations provided for, leading to censure by the assistant judge advocate general. Meanwhile, in the camp's toxic environment, interethnic squabbles turned into full-scale brawls, resulting in serious injuries. But the single greatest menace was the cold. In the open encampment, which consisted of canvas tents, the fierce weather proved challenging. In early fall, temperatures hovered around freezing, and the first snow fell on 17 October. Throughout that month, some 180 prisoners were assigned to roadwork each day, but by the first week of November and the onset of severe cold, only a handful were sent out to clear snow and cut firewood for the camp. Retreating to Banff once more seemed a sensible if not life-saving course of action.

A return to the old quarters at Banff had been discussed in the fall, but, given the unknowns, a final decision was delayed. The diplomatic dispute with Germany continued to dog Canadian officials, complicating the issue of what kind of future awaited the internees. Then there was industry's appetite for more workers, which also led to indecision. Would the Castle camp be emptied, thereby obviating the question of relocation? This was a political matter to be decided independently of the circumstances facing the camp. In practical terms, however, by the first week of November, extreme weather made any further delay dangerous. Once the internment director granted authority, the camp was quickly packed up and the prisoners transferred to Banff. The move was fortuitous. "Banff looked mighty good to both guards and internees," the *Crag and Canyon* reported, noting that temperatures "flirted with the 37 below zero [Fahrenheit] mark and it was an utter impossibility to maintain any appreciable degree of heat in the tents – unless one had a relay of batmen at one's disposal."[39]

The denizens of Castle camp were glad to return to Banff, but the townsfolk of Banff were not so enthusiastic. The local paper lamented the fact that little economic benefit had been derived from the operation since provisioning was almost entirely conducted through Calgary, whose Conservative association had greater influence. The reduced size of the camp was also noted, suggesting that even less value would result from the now smaller operation. In the opinion of the *Crag*, however, it did not matter, the paper dismissing the prisoners as a blight that the community would do well to be rid of: "Their diminished number will not be greatly deplored, especially as the majority of our citizens are of the opinion that the scenic outlook is not vastly improved by the presence of the slouching, bovine-faced foreigners."[40] The paper's sneering characterization of the inmates reflected not only latent xenophobia but also active local hostility towards the prisoners, inflamed, at least in part, by the disheartening news that the affable and well-liked Francis Eykelbosh, a resident of nearby Canmore and former guard at the Banff/Castle Mountain camp, had succumbed to his wounds on the Western Front. Shocked that someone they knew had been killed – and by an enemy whose kindred were interned at Banff – local opinion was now solidly against the enemy alien. There was no room for sympathy.

During an inspection by the military district's commanding officer, internees lodged complaints of brutal treatment by guards. Upon learning of the protests, the *Crag and Canyon* editors remarked that these "foreign scum" were "best handled with a pickaxe handle."[41] Meanwhile, the bayoneting of a prisoner who refused to walk faster on his way to work was fobbed off as a minor incident. Little was also made of the suicide of prisoner George Budak, who, from the moment he was arrested, stubbornly insisted that he was innocent and had nothing to do with the war. His pleas ignored, Budak surrendered to melancholy and despair, taking a razor to his throat and abdomen during the night of the Christmas Vigil. The *Crag* spoke disparagingly of the inconvenience presented by this tragedy as citizens were "yank[ed] from their firesides on Christmas Eve to serve on the coroner's jury."[42] There could be no charity for those deemed to be enemies, and camp authorities were encouraged to exercise resolve by a public clamouring for retribution.

Despite the *Crag*'s assertion that no benefit was to be derived from relocating the prisoners to Banff, they did in fact perform invaluable service. The Parks Branch had set out ambitious plans for the winter season, assigning the prisoners to projects that would improve local infrastructure and enhance Banff's potential as a winter sporting venue. From mid-January to the end of March, approximately 140 were sent out daily to straighten the corkscrew road leading up to the top of Tunnel Mountain with its panoramic view of town and valley. A group was put to work constructing a large retaining rock wall and viewing site at the foot of the Bow Falls, while others built a ski run and toboggan glide. Prisoners were also assigned to smaller projects undertaken by private interests to improve the recreation facilities of the park: cutting trails for the Alpine Club of Canada; reclaiming land for a shooting range; and, with the onset of spring, ploughing a large tract for growing hay to feed the horses used for leisure riding in the park. Then there was the enormous winter carnival ice palace, created for the pleasure and amusement of the local citizenry.[43] Internment labour was available and there for the taking – a principle that invited requests from a variety of sources, both public and private.

Indeed, once it became known that prisoners could be made available if work was guaranteed, industry quickly turned to the internees as a ready and inexpensive labour pool. Such applications led to regular paroles, at first individually and later in pairs or more. Over time, requests from industry for larger groups of prisoners were received. On 16 April 1917 the nearby Canmore Coal Company applied for more than fifty men. This was followed by an appeal from the Canadian Pacific Railway for all the prisoners in the camp. These and other requests were unexpected but favourably received in so far as the problem of enemy alien joblessness – the principal reason behind their internment – was being addressed. Still, the internees were enemy aliens and only those judged to be compliant would be paroled. Security, in effect, continued to be a consideration.[44]

The tension in the internees' status of being both civilians and POWs echoed in the vacillating decision making regarding their release. As civilians they could be paroled to the extent that jobs were available. As war prisoners, however, they still needed to be carefully screened and handled, especially as this related to the conditions and terms of their parole. Thus, when it was learned that workers at Canmore were engaged in a strike, the plan to release ten internees to the mine was shelved for fear that they might add to the trouble there. On the other hand, when the CPR guaranteed work and provided assurances that there were no labour issues at the company, a total of 109 men, considered acceptable, were paroled in the final week of April. Meanwhile, anxiety gripped those who were passed over. Sensing misfortune, some attempted flight. On 7 June a prisoner bolted from the Hot Springs work gang, with guards giving chase and shots being fired. A few weeks later, another prisoner working at the barracks slipped away unnoticed during a favourable moment.

The last desperate escapes underlined what was known to all: the operations at Banff were winding down. The prospect of being deported, regarding which rumours were rife, persuaded those who remained to take a last chance at escape. In the meantime, the business of internment continued, although the imminent closure of the camp brought some urgency to completing projects that were still outstanding. In a final effort to make use of their labour, internees were put to work on extending the back nine holes of the golf course at the Banff Springs Hotel.[45] It was felt that, if this opportunity were passed up, the golf course would not get done, at least not for the foreseeable future. Accordingly, the internees were rushed to the site. Shortly after the project was completed, the remaining forty-seven prisoners were gathered up and, in the company of twenty-five guards and non-commissioned officers, sent to the distant Kapuskasing internment camp in northern Ontario to await their fate. In July 1917 the camp was shuttered, and so ended the story of First World War internment at Banff/Castle Mountain.

At the war's start, because of the potential risk they represented, aliens of enemy origin were identified for possible internment as POWs under the provisions of the War Measures Act. Internment, however, soon devolved into something else as the issue of the large number of jobless and impoverished enemy aliens became a concern. Internment would prove useful in dealing with this issue since its legitimacy as a war measure was unassailable. There could be no questioning internment's role or purpose, and this made it politically attractive. But there were also extenuating factors that led to its appeal. The opportunity to utilize the prisoners as a reliable and inexpensive source of labour on several projects crucial to the development of the national parks factored into the final decision to create internment camps in Canada's mountain interior.

What occurred at Banff/Castle Mountain, then, followed from the twin impulses of utility and ambition. More important, it mirrored the willingness of officials to sidestep a sobering ethical-political question: What obligations and rights were owed to these people as recent arrivals and civilians? This could not be easily answered except in a perfunctory way. Thus, as aliens of enemy nationality, and in the context of war, these people were seen as de facto enemies, sidelining the issue of their standing as innocent civilians. Meanwhile, their internment as POWs carried with it the presumption that they would work and, if necessary, that they would be forced to do so. This was a fact of considerable significance given the level of public hostility, resentment, and suspicion. Viewed through this lens – where their status as civilian POWs was vague (and therefore politically advantageous) – the practice of internment would take shape.

As outsiders and perceived adversaries, those behind barbed wire were treated harshly. The details of what occurred at Banff/Castle Mountain speak to this reality – a cruelty that was surpassed only by the enormity of the ambition behind it. Despite the war, a time when funds for public works were scarce, the infrastructure of the park would be developed no matter the cost. More accurately, it was through utilizing the labour of those whom the war had made victims that the park was able to be developed at all. The internees would work because, designated as POWs, this was required of them. And so the stage was set for those tasked with their oversight. Their goal was simple: put the prisoners to work and prevent them from escaping. That the internees were civilians made no difference since officers and guards alike felt the prisoners were the cause of their own private hardship. Thus, the internees were neglected and even became the objects of personal grievances, underscoring the moral and even psychological danger in which Canada's military was placed by both the ideology behind and consequences of internment.

Both in terms of operation and conditions, the Banff/Castle Mountain camp was indistinguishable from other frontier internment camps. Still, the appearance of prisoners trudging through the Banff townsite under military guard and being forcibly put to work stood in stark contrast to the belief that the national park was a place of rest, recovery, and renewal. That this contrast did not register could only follow from the belief that the internees were enemies and, therefore, their treatment required no explanation.

On the other hand, for the internees at the Banff/Castle Mountain camp, their predicament was simply inexplicable. They could never have expected this. They had come to the country in good faith, yet they were imprisoned. Facing intolerable conditions, scores would flee from a situation that was completely baffling to them. Made out to be war prisoners and treated abominably, they asked what they had done to deserve this and what was to become of them. These disquieting questions remained unanswered. Meanwhile, for the curious few who visited, what went on in the camp was of little concern: after all, they were enemies.

In silence, the internees suffered. Their anguish was intensified by their isolation in the mountain wilderness. Forlorn and forgotten, their sense of abandonment was palpable. Not a few were overcome by depression and despair, having lost hope in a place that, paradoxically, had been created to be a comfort to the nation. The irony, of course, was thick and the betrayal deep, and the experience bordered on the surreal. But it was also fated, given that those sent to Canada's Banff National Park were increasingly seen as unwanted and unwelcome.

6

Kapuskasing

Internment on Ontario's Northern Frontier, 1915–20

Watson Kirkconnell was scheduled to depart for Europe in 1916 as a fledgling captain with the Canadian Expeditionary Force. Prevented from going overseas at the last minute because of a medical condition, he chose nevertheless to remain in the military, serving with the Internment Directorate as paymaster at Kapuskasing, an internment camp in Canada's hinterland. Mustered out at war's end and foreshadowing his later career as a scholar, Kirkconnell penned two articles about the experience.[1] Spending years in the wilderness on an operation that garnered little attention or respect, it was an opportunity for him to share his story. The writing was cathartic. But he also believed it was a tale worth telling.

As Kirkconnell narrated, in the vast boreal forest of Ontario's north – situated at the intersection of the newly built Transcontinental Railway and the Kapuskasing River, hundreds of kilometres from civilization in any direction – a collection of POWs was put to work carving out of the wilds a place of future settlement. It was a scheme born of an audacious idea. The region's flat topography, high water table, and rich clay soil was thought to hold agricultural promise. If properly prepared, this fertile land could lure future colonists to the area. The scheme spoke to imagination, ambition, and grit. Kirkconnell sought to convey all of this. But he also communicated the difficulties associated with the project, such as the resistance of the prisoners to their work. Indeed, he described at length the antagonism and resentments built up by years spent behind Canadian barbed wire. Still, for Kirkconnell, this was war, and they were prisoners – a battle of wills was to be expected.

This perspective, however, also prevented the young captain from delivering a more clear-eyed account of the experience. Aware that the internees were non-combatants, he failed to ask: How was it that these civilians became POWs in the first place? Moreover, like so many others, he was indifferent to their protests that, even though they were migrants originating from countries now at war with the British Empire, they were not adversaries and showed no malice towards Canada. Nor did he appear to make much of the fact that a significant number of them would be deported at war's end. An officer of junior rank, he was naturally dissuaded from making inquiries. Because Kirkconnell ignored these and other matters, the result was an incomplete if not skewed interpretation of the events that occurred at Kapuskasing.

How, then, should Kapuskasing be understood? At a certain level, the experience mirrored the objectives of a government bent on a policy of internment. But what was behind the policy rationale that would see immigrants turned into POWs, and what did it mean for civilians to be sent to work as war prisoners in Canada's hinterland? What were the motivations of those who would use their labour? And what effect did this have on the outlook of the military personnel charged with overseeing civilian immigrants in a remote area, away from inquiring eyes?

These were the considerations that defined the Kapuskasing internment experience, paralleling developments found elsewhere in Canada as part of the country's broader internment operation. But Kapuskasing was unique in that the camp continued to function until 1920, when the Treaty of Versailles was signed, well after other internment sites had been shuttered. Serving as a place of consolidation, Kapuskasing held prisoners prior to their being removed from the country. What was the intent behind this? Why were some prisoners released and others detained indefinitely, and what did this reveal about the evolving role and meaning of internment?

The story of Kapuskasing concerns both the general and the particular: how the policy of internment fundamentally shaped the experience there and how specific considerations gave the experience a distinctive quality. In this sense Kapuskasing is a story that goes far beyond the account authored by Captain Kirkconnell, who described it simply as a place where nature and the will of the enemy were tamed. Kapuskasing was where people were forced to labour because of who they were said to be and what they represented. In the context of war, the fact that they had been invited into Canada meant nothing. That they were civilians mattered even less. Confined until the coming of the peace, they would eventually be expelled as the unwanted. In the end, Kapuskasing spoke to their predicament, laying bear the story of the cruel logic of internment in Canada during the Great War.

Eleven days after Canada's entry into the First World War, the government issued a Royal Proclamation that focused on security issues, not least of which was preventing reservists from returning to their homelands where they might take up arms. Security was a legitimate concern and internment a necessary corollary of this unease. But official apprehension extended beyond the problem posed by universal mobilization. War with the British Empire placed those who originated from belligerent lands in the unenviable role of aliens of enemy origin, elevating public suspicion and fuelling rumours of disloyalty. With an economy in flux because of war, and with resentment being widespread, thousands of enemy aliens were dismissed from their places of work. With so many unemployed and destitute, Ottawa became increasingly concerned, especially as winter approached.

Steps were taken, therefore, to address the situation, including issuing Order-in-Council PC 2721 under the War Measures Act, which required enemy aliens to register with local authorities and indicate whether they had sufficient means to remain in the country. Those enemy aliens identified as being without resources would be interned as POWs. An unconventional measure, it necessarily would lead to judgments about who these people were and to decisions regarding how they were to be treated. Still, the impulse to contain the enemy alien problem, which had been cast as a security issue, was being addressed. Indeed, with emergency powers in hand, thousands of enemy aliens – unemployed, homeless, and poor – were arrested and processed for internment as war prisoners.

It soon became apparent that municipal jails (serving as holding facilities) and military prisons (such as Fort Henry in Kingston and the Citadel in Halifax) would not suffice. The swell in numbers made alternative sites a priority, convincing the newly appointed internment director, Major General William Otter, to search for partners in a quest to reduce the mounting costs associated with internment. The dominion Department of Agriculture had for some time expressed interest in exploring the growing potential of the clay belt in northern Ontario and concluded that an experimental farm could be created to attract settlers to the area. This idea was of long-standing interest to the Ontario premier, William Hearst, who, while also serving as the minister responsible for immigration and colonization, was a strong advocate for developing Ontario's north. But it was a project the province could not undertake unilaterally – certainly not under the austerity conditions brought on by war. POW labour, therefore, presented an opportunity, and the premier recognized it as such.[2]

The plan was for the Department of Agriculture to offer expertise as well as to cover the cost of POW labour to clear forests for farming. The military, under the authority of the Internment Directorate, would guard and maintain the prisoners. For its part, the province would provide land and assume responsibility for overseeing the cutting of trees and millwork. As for the profit from the sale of lumber, this would be shared between the province and agriculture department. Seeing a potential windfall, Premier Hearst boasted that the model farm could be established without cost to the province, apart from its providing a land concession of some one thousand acres.

Hearst would not be denied the benefits from this pool of labour, which, in his view "would only be limited practically by the ability to provide work and accommodation."[3] That the dominion Department of Agriculture approached the government of Quebec served as a further impetus. In this regard, the premier insisted that Ontario simply "wanted its full share of Austrian and German prisoners of war for this work."[4] Underlining the premier's indifference to their plight, the prisoners were regarded as a spoil of war. The only condition set was that the project be located at a distance from the Quebec camp so as to minimize future competition for homesteaders. A grant of 1,282 acres was offered by the province of Ontario. With that, negotiations were concluded regarding the creation of an internment station at Kapuskasing.

On 10 January 1915, the first contingent of fifty-six POWs arrived from Fort Henry. They were immediately put to work erecting bunkhouses. Shortly thereafter, the commanding officer, Major Fredrick Clarke, advised district headquarters that a hundred prisoners could be received weekly, with sleeping quarters available for four hundred. By March, a total of 438 POWs were at Kapuskasing, easing Fort Henry of its surplus. The majority were Austro-Hungarian subjects, consisting of minorities from the periphery of the empire – Ukrainians, Croats, Poles, and others – part of the great wave of turn-of-the-century migration to Canada. To this number were added prisoners of German and Ottoman origin. In the main, all were labourers, unemployed, and indigent. Now under military guard, they were expected to work.

Results were soon realized. Officials of the agriculture department were apprised in April that seventy-five acres of dense forest had been cut down. Mills in the vicinity were notified that four hundred cords of pulpwood and three thousand logs were available for purchase, with the promise of more to come. Work was also undertaken to construct military barracks, work sheds, and more bunkhouses for new prisoners, who arrived daily. Upon inspection, Commissioner J.F. Whitson, of the Ontario government's Northern Development Branch, described the site as "a thriving village" and praised the work as first-rate, enthusing that "the beauty of the place" was slowly being revealed with the removal of the trees.[5] Premier Hearst, however, was more sagacious in his assessment of Kapuskasing. With a captive labour force, costs were minimal. Sensing an even greater opportunity with the arrival of more prisoners, he proposed that they be employed on clearing additional land adjacent to the Transcontinental Railway. Two satellite camps were soon established at a distance from the main station.

The scale of the Kapuskasing operation was impressive. By August 1915, Toronto's *Empire and Mail* estimated that fourteen hundred prisoners were clearing land at a per-prisoner cost of just twenty-five cents a day – the allotted military wage for supplementary non-military work. In the newspaper's judgment, this was a good investment, especially since the prisoners were compliant.[6] The satisfaction was short-lived, however, the *Empire* soon reporting several escapes from the camp. Given the risks involved, flight signalled desperation, underscoring the reality that, for some, the conditions were simply too much to bear.

That the conditions were gruelling, there could be no doubt. The pace of felling and milling trees was, in fact, relentless, with no prospect of let-up. From 1 May to 20 July, some 8,818 logs were cut and prepared. Another 4,810 logs followed between 20 July and 1 September, resulting in 1,567,605 board feet of lumber. To the job of clearing land for farm use, road construction was also added. By January 1916, in the nearby townships of O'Brien, Fauquier, Owens, and Williamson, 124 acres of dense black spruce were cut, and thirty-five miles grubbed and graded in preparation for a future motorway. Twelve culverts and one bridge were also constructed as part of the project.

Almost from the outset, Germany registered protests with the UK government after receiving reports from neutral American consular officials tasked with monitoring conditions faced by internees in camps across Canada, including Kapuskasing.[7] Although the public viewed the internees at Kapuskasing and elsewhere as war prisoners, they were in fact interned civilians.[8] International law, however, was unclear as to their rights since little consideration was given to the prospect of massively interning enemy alien civilians who had no direct involvement in the conflict. In the absence of international juridical guidance, rationalizations were offered as to why they were designated POWs and put to work. Officials in Canada's Department of Justice, for instance, claimed that, since "the country of their allegiance" made no provision for their maintenance, the status of POW would apply. It was further rationalized: "That they should be accorded treatment [as] prisoners of war obviously works to the advantage to these distressed people rather than as a hardship."[9] The *Montreal Gazette* seconded this line of thought, commenting: "It is likely that most of them will have a far better time of it as prisoners than they would have had … as alien enemies out of money and work."[10]

At Kapuskasing, quotas were set as provincial overseers looked to ensure that funds were properly used. Efficiency became a priority after Department of Agriculture officials gave notice that the ministry would no longer cover the prisoner allowance since the lands necessary for the experimental farm had been cleared. This prompted the Ontario government – anxious not to lose access to the labour – to pay for the continued use of the internees on roadwork and other projects, but only at the assigned POW rate. Premier Hearst stipulated: "we will only take labour when we want it, and … we will not be compelled to retain any labourers on the work that are not satisfactory for us."[11] The premier was adamant: "We could not afford to pay 25¢ per day in the winter time, nor would we want to pay for any class of men they may want to send to us." The availability of cheap POW labour was an opportunity. But in Hearst's judgment, the numbers also had to add up. The role of internment was now delineated by economic considerations, making policy reassessment unlikely.

In view of these added priorities, quarrels over the quantity and quality of work were frequent. Provincial overseers insisted the pace of work be maintained. To ensure that there would be no slackening and to minimize cost overruns, the guards at Kapuskasing were encouraged to exercise strict discipline in managing the internees. This, however, demanded that guards and officers be suited to the job. All along, the camp's commandant, Major Clarke, insisted that the calibre of recruits assigned to Kapuskasing be adequate to coping with the physically and psychologically demanding conditions. The difficulty, for Clarke, was that the camp's most capable personnel, while on leave, were often pilfered for overseas duty. To put the camp on a more rational basis, Clarke insisted either this practice be stopped or, alternatively, similarly competent replacements be provided.

Quality of personnel was a particularly sensitive issue with Clarke since recruits of questionable value were being sent to Kapuskasing.[12] Some failed their medical examinations; others, having returned traumatized from the European front, behaved erratically. A few of the enlistments were even of "enemy" birth, albeit naturalized. Meanwhile, the senior ranks were populated with men of dubious character or questionable ability, including the camp's medical officer, who, it was felt, might still be of use, despite his demotion to the rank of private for his propensity to drink. And then there were those individuals who simply did not want to be in a place that had no apparent connection to the struggle overseas. They had enlisted to fight and took exception to the job of guarding civilians, even those of enemy origin. In the end, the quality and mindset of both guards and officers reflected the standing of the operation. Internment was of little military importance, and those sent to Kapuskasing were under no illusion that this was the case.

All this fed into an atmosphere of resentment, which resulted in bitterness, abuses, and irregularities at Kapuskasing. Punishment diets – bread and water – as well as solitary confinement were administered liberally for any infraction, large or small, while the lack of discipline among the guards resulted in alarming displays of intimidation and brutality. Allegations of abuse were brought to the attention of the internment director, Major General Otter, who sought to put a stop to the more egregious violations. For Otter, nothing was to be gained by the wanton physical mistreatment of POWs, which he condemned as a failure of moral character. "The object of their present duties are rendered valueless, and the good name of Canada brought to the level of the Hun," he declared.[13] But the director also understood that, in the wilderness, there was little he could do if immediate and proper supervision was lacking.

In November 1915, an American consular representative reported that the mood at the frontier internment camps was tense and the prisoners surly. The offences being committed, from the petty to the serious, added to the misery and sullenness of the stations, including Kapuskasing. It was not surprising, then, that attempted escapes at the northern Ontario facility were on the rise or that personnel, anxious to quit the hard-luck camp, pleaded for discharges. When the appeals of the latter were refused, once on leave they simply disappeared. Others, however, patiently looked to be reassigned, among these the commanding officer of Kapuskasing – Major Clarke – whose repeated requests for a transfer would eventually be approved.

Clarke's replacement was Lieutenant Colonel George Royce, who, it was felt, having served some twenty-five years as an officer with the Queen's Own Rifles, had the necessary command experience. But Royce also possessed an anxious disposition, exacerbated by the challenges he faced. When he assumed the post in January 1916, Royce immediately expressed his uneasiness about the camp, which at this time contained some twelve hundred prisoners. Like his predecessor, he complained to district headquarters about the quality of the guards. Many had no experience or knowledge of what guarding entailed, while others were without any military training at all. Royce explained that, at Kapuskasing, each single guard had in his charge many prisoners, a duty requiring men of experience.[14] For the lieutenant colonel, this was no small matter. He understood that there were expectations and the failure to meet these would reflect badly on his command.

Indeed, it was anticipated that the prisoners would work steadily and deliver value. To this end, the progress of the work and expenditures were closely scrutinized.[15] Invariably, discrepancies in the accounts would occur. For the month of February 1916, the value of internment labour at Kapuskasing amounted to $2,253.50. The Northern Development Branch officials, however, estimated the cost of the work at $1,536.25. This inconsistency, which translated into a shortfall of some 2,869 man-days of labour, was attributed to religious holidays (which internment authorities were obliged to respect) and sickness (real and feigned). Since in these cases the prisoners were idle, provincial authorities insisted that they would not be paid. They were expected to work, and if they did not, then the Internment Directorate was responsible for any deficit that might result. In the context of an operation experiencing rising costs, Royce was under pressure to ensure that the prisoners were being used to maximum effect. There could be no delays, stoppages, or interruptions.

To offset criticism and give credence to the idea that there was still merit to the operation, Royce emphasized the camp's accomplishments. Beyond the six hundred acres that had been stumped and slashed for agricultural use, he reported in March 1916 that no fewer than five hundred men were working daily on logging and clearing bush, resulting in an additional eighteen miles of roads being cleared and graded under his command. Some eight thousand feet of commercial-grade lumber was also being produced every day at the sawmill. In correspondence with his superiors, Royce communicated: "this camp is worth seeing, and it would surprise you, the magnitude of the operations."[16] But, more important, Royce gave assurance regarding one of the proposed plans for Kapuskasing – however bizarre – that the prisoners, released at the end of the war, would be able to purchase lots for sale and occupy the land as future colonists. He and others were convinced that once the internees recognized and appreciated the value of what they had accomplished, they would willingly take up settlement.[17] The idea that the internees could be both enemy prisoners and future colonists did not appear to strike the commander as odd or incongruous. What mattered was that the work be undertaken, and the assignment completed.

Despite Royce's enthusiasm for the project, there was no hiding the problems with which Kapuskasing was beset. Maintaining discipline was a constant worry given the pressures of the camp. Conflict – between guards and prisoners, military administrators and provincial overseers, and among the internees themselves – was endemic. All were in close confinement, and the environment was toxic. "We have fights among prisoners occasionally, as they are not all lambs," the commandant commented, "and if they cannot fight with anyone else, they fight amongst themselves."[18] With tensions rising, Royce, believing that all military personnel were needed, declined applications for overseas deployment and refused any furloughs. Sensing trouble, he insisted the camp be supplied with more ammunition, writing to his superiors: "While disturbances, so far, have been of a minor nature, it is liable to be serious at any time."[19]

There was good reason for Royce to feel unnerved. The winter of 1916 proved to be unduly harsh, with daily temperatures hovering between minus forty and minus fifty degrees Fahrenheit. Prisoners complained of the bitter cold. Frostbite was commonplace.

Frozen timber could not be easily hewn, making the work dangerous. Infirmary records reveal a plethora of cold-related mishaps, including hacked hands and feet.[20] Among the guards, the ability to stand watch in this inhospitable climate for long stretches at a time tested even the most able. And then there was the simple risk of guarding prisoners in close quarters who were in possession of a range of tools – axes, picks, pikes, shovels, and hammers. The stress among the guards reinforced the antipathy directed towards their charges. To address the strain, Royce requested more men. His application, however, was rejected, pending a policy reassessment regarding the release of prisoners to industry.

Royce's fears were soon realized. A decision had been made early in May 1916 to close the internment camp at Petawawa, with most prisoners being paroled to industry. The remaining two hundred prisoners, considered troublesome, were transferred to Kapuskasing from Petawawa for safekeeping. Arriving at Kapuskasing, they carried their grievances with them and, thus, were in a state of agitation. Within days, the internees refused to accept their work assignments, protesting the compulsory nature of the work. Sixty were singled out for solitary confinement, and, when they were gathered for escort, a crowd of prisoners blocked their seizure. As the troops assembled, more prisoners joined in. Despite warning shots and pistol whippings, the prisoners did not disperse and gave no sign of retreating. The soldiers at the command charged the crowd of three hundred with bayonets drawn, and the prisoners were eventually driven back to their bunkhouses. In the confusion, reports indicated that several prisoners were shot and killed. In the end, twelve were seriously injured.[21]

As Royce reported, the trouble could have been much worse if most prisoners had not been turned out for work earlier that day. He expected further disturbances and requested that a machine-gun squadron be attached to the guard: "It might never be required, but it would certainly have a moral effect on the prisoners."[22]

Royce insisted that the internees' chief complaint concerned compulsory labour and the apparent discrepancy pertaining to that issue: some were compelled to work while others were given special dispensation as "first-class prisoners." Unless the policy were to be amended, prisoner resentment could not be easily contained, and even the most basic of tasks, Royce felt, would not be carried out without the use of force. This, he was convinced, would only lead to further violent clashes.

Royce's concerns were shared. The district officer commanding, Brigadier General Logie, wrote to the internment director saying that the implementation of the policy of compulsory labour was problematic. In his opinion, it was unfair not to provide the commandant with more definitive instructions as to whether the prisoners could be forced to work. But, as Major General Otter observed: "The question is one that it has not been advisable to promulgate any definite order upon, as there is no regulation compelling them to do so, while on the other hand it is better both for themselves and the public that they should. Therefore, the matter has been left to the tact and judgment of Commandants and until now no trouble has ever been experienced."[23] In the absence of clear instructions, Royce pleaded, once again, for more men, He requested that forty-one more be added to the existing 219.

While preliminary authority was given to increase the guard, the recruiting depot in Toronto conveyed that, given the rate of remuneration, it was impossible to find individuals willing to go north. Kapuskasing was a hardship post with little to recommend it. To mollify the commander, Royce was informed that the more efficient Mark II version of the aging Ross rifle would be issued to guards at the camp. However, when told that no additional soldiers would be sent his way despite the difficulties he faced, Royce indicated that, if not reassigned, he would resign. Royce's transfer was granted. He relinquished command on 17 July 1916, the same day that forest fires threatened the nearby settlements of Cochrane, Kelso, and Iroquois Falls. In his last act as commander, Royce sent prisoners and guards to help extinguish the raging infernos. Together, they fought the flames and gave assistance, but not before the great Matheson Fire of northern Ontario claimed the lives of 223 local inhabitants.

Lieutenant Colonel W.H. Rodden was chosen to replace Royce. Rodden's appointment followed his earlier posting at the sizeable Spirit Lake camp near Abitibi, Quebec, which was to close permanently because of consolidation. Across the country, camps were shuttered due to the growing number of internees who were being paroled in response to economic demand. Since April 1916, appeals for labourers had been fielded by industry and agriculture, hurriedly looking to secure replacements for native-born workers who had enlisted. POW labour at the Kapuskasing and Spirit Lake camps was seen as a potential resource in northern Ontario and Quebec. Applications from a range of companies necessarily followed, including the Canadian Pacific Railway. On 2 June 1916, the CPR asked for no fewer than a thousand internees from Kapuskasing to work on the Lake Superior Division line.

The government was disposed to release the prisoners to satisfy demand. But it was also mindful of the potential repercussions of doing so. After all, the government had introduced the category of enemy alien, thereby laying the foundation for the public's perception that these people were in fact enemies. Yet originally, for Ottawa, the internment of enemy aliens had centred on indigence, thus linking the issue of security to employment status. So, to the degree that their status would change with a job offer, thereby restoring their original function in the economy, their release could be envisaged. However, this would occur only under certain conditions. The prisoners had to demonstrate their eligibility for parole, which meant that only those who were amenable to working where assigned would be discharged. They would also be paid free labour wages so as not to undermine the existing labour market. And finally, like the wider enemy alien population, they would have to register and report regularly to local officials.

Public resentment and suspicion, unsurprisingly, was difficult to overcome. The thought of working alongside released POWs was unimaginable, resulting in calls for the government to abandon its plans of shuttering the camps and for all enemy aliens in the country to be interned. In Ontario, native-born workers mobilized "to drive out of town interned aliens who had been brought in to address the labour shortage."[24] Unbeknownst to the public, however, the policy of internment was proving untenable. Germany had long protested the compulsory use of civilian internees on work projects in Canada and even threatened retaliation against British prisoners in German camps. This made it difficult for the government to continue with the policy as originally conceived, especially with pressure emanating from London, which for some time had feared reprisals.[25]

From the outset, internment had been conducted with local needs in mind. However, the reality of a world at war made it part of a global undertaking. Internment in Canada was connected to an imperial network that imposed responsibilities on those employing the practice.[26] In the context of the Great War, these local and global dimensions were not easily separated, refuting the idea that internment in Canada was a purely domestic affair. Thus, in addition to changing economic conditions, pressures upon Canada to align its practice with imperial policy necessitated that Canadian internment be modified. As a result, Kapuskasing, as well as other camps, would slowly be emptied of their prisoners when pressure from London and domestic economic demand rendered their internment unsustainable or impractical, at least in the manner it was originally designed. By late August 1916, only seventy-five internees remained at Kapuskasing.

Camps across the country were quickly closed. Yet within each there remained those who were not easily reconciled and, continuing to be recalcitrant, made their resentments known. At Kapuskasing, the remaining prisoners, still compelled to work, drove railway spikes into the logs, damaging the mill's saws. These and other acts of defiance were seen as signs of rebelliousness, the handiwork of those who could not be reintegrated. They remained interned at Kapuskasing while those from other camps who resisted were also sent there, where they would be held until their fate could be determined. Kapuskasing's isolation, capacity to intern large numbers, and proximity to transport made it a preferred location.[27] Given the perceived danger that the large number of new arrivals would pose, instructions were issued to reinforce the existing wire compound at Kapuskasing with two additional tall fences, set six feet apart, around the perimeter. Completed in May 1917, the system of fences was described as a "band of steel." Shortly thereafter, 250 internees were transferred from Spirit Lake upon its closure, while another four hundred prisoners arrived from Fort Henry in Kingston.

Within days of their arrival at Kapuskasing, two inmates escaped. Given the recent security improvements, the news of the escapes convinced Major General Otter that there were underlying problems with the camp administration. Inquiries revealed irregularities on the part of the new commander, Lieutenant Colonel Rodden, reinforcing Otter's suspicions, especially after other, earlier transgressions attracted the internment director's attention. During a surprise visit to the Spirit Lake camp immediately prior to its closure, Otter found eleven hundred cords of stowed wood at the nearby railway siding. The large stack was unaccounted for in either the work or pay schedules. Upon subsequent investigation, the source of the wood was identified as trees that had been cut on property adjacent to the camp. This land, it was further discovered, was owned by Rodden – the commandant of Spirit Lake at the time. Only recently reassigned to Kapuskasing, Rodden vehemently denied wrongdoing, asserting that the prisoners had strayed onto his property.

The impropriety, however, could not be overlooked. Coupled with news of the recent escapes, Rodden was quietly relieved of his new command, a position he originally held through the Department of Justice.[28]

A disappointment to Otter, such an offence was not all that uncommon. Similar incidents took place at other camps – the result of officers of dubious quality and character being foisted on the directorate through connections and influence. But it was also a function of the uncertain status of the internees. These were enemies and their treatment was apparently of little consequence, a notion reinforced by the camp's remoteness. Why, otherwise, would they have been sent to such a place, neglected, and ignored? This was a question that provided motive to those who saw the opportunity for private gain. Rodden was one among many who looked to benefit personally from the misery of the internees – individuals who, effectively, were without protection.

Internment at Fort Henry ended with the removal of the prisoners to Kapuskasing, enabling the Fort Henry commandant, Lieutenant Colonel W.E. Date, to replace the disgraced Rodden in May 1917. Date was an officious man. But as a disciplinarian, Major General Otter also saw in him the traits needed to finally bring the camp to order.[29] Knowing of his reputation, but putting aside any misgivings, Otter made the conscious decision to appoint Date. He would not be disappointed. Upon taking command, Date immediately put the troops on notice that regulations would be strictly observed, and that lax performance of duty would have consequences. Among the internees, a program of stringent inspections and curfews was introduced, as were new austerity measures. When Canada's food comptroller urged Canadians to decrease food consumption, and as British officials had stated that internees in Canadian camps were liberally fed relative to British POWs in German camps, Date strictly enforced a policy of reduced rations at Kapuskasing.

Not only was Date domineering and inflexible, but he was also suspicious. In the main, he considered his charges to be treacherous – an attitude that laid bare his unwholesome prejudices and fears. It also, however, spoke to circumstances. The government's original description of immigrants from Germany and Austria-Hungary as individuals with questionable allegiances helped frame Date's attitude towards them. No quarter was to be given the presumed enemy, and Date, resolute in his duty, was unapologetic in treating them as such.[30] There were, however, parameters – especially as Germany, ever watchful, was attentive to the welfare of its co-nationals abroad. These two realities, potentially at odds, portended conflict.

Germany, in its diplomatic engagement with Britain, had long held that civilian internees could not be forced to work, although it accepted the principle of voluntary work if the rate of pay approximated that earned by free labour. Thus, as of 15 June 1917, those paroled to the railways, but still required to report, were paid twenty cents per hour. However, for British officials and, by extension, Canadian authorities, it was expected that those who remained behind barbed wire would perform extended duties (including cutting wood for the camp) at the POW rate of twenty-five cents per day. This led to a diplomatic dispute. Berlin was adamant: work that took prisoners outside the camp (even cutting firewood) was compulsory in nature and therefore in violation of norms. Meanwhile, the internees at Kapuskasing, implacable in their attitude towards camp authority, took their cue from this political quarrel, claiming that they would not work at the direction of the camp administration under any circumstances.

Date interpreted the prisoners' refusal to work as a challenge to his command.[31] More immediately, his frustration centred on the problem posed by their refusal: how to prepare the camp before the onset of winter. Firewood had to be obtained from the bush and cut for the camp. Being as it was for the welfare of the camp and the prisoners' own health, the commandant felt that, under the Hague Convention, this type of work was the responsibility of the prisoners. The difficulty lay in interpretation. Did fatigue duties outside the camp constitute compulsory labour and therefore violate the understanding under the regulations regarding POWs, let alone norms that might apply to interned civilians?[32]

The result was an impasse that led to a build-up of tensions, especially as relief funds provided by the German government incentivized prisoners not to comply with the commandant's orders. In response, for those who refused to work, Date proposed withholding their allowance from those who refused to work, "inasmuch as a prisoner could earn almost as much by idleness as by industry."[33] The reduced rations were cut even more. The militants reciprocated by severely beating prisoners who chose to comply, thereby putting a halt to all work at Kapuskasing. This, in turn, prompted the lieutenant colonel to confront the instigators, forcing them into isolation cells at the point of a revolver while placing troops at the ready to address the threat of an uprising. Date was convinced that only strong measures would prevail. He personally felt that the recent shooting of a prisoner who had resisted had its desired effect on the strikers: "mak[ing] them realize what they are up against."[34] He was wrong. The prisoners remained defiant and declared that they would not capitulate, even in the face of cold weather, starvation, and the continued use of threats and violence.

On the face of it, the conflict was a test of wills. More profoundly, the stalemate derived from a fundamental difference regarding the rights of civilian prisoners. For the internees, nothing less than the observance of norms would suffice; only in this way could they retain their dignity and self-worth. They insisted that the dictates of natural justice and international law be followed.[35] For Date, on the other hand, by disregarding camp regulations, the prisoners proved themselves to be no more than rabble and malcontents undeserving of the protections afforded under the laws of war. He dismissed all representations by the internees as being the work "of troublemakers, obstructionists, agitators, who are always talking 'Hague Rules,' etc."[36]

The political and psychological chasm between Date and the internees made it unlikely the situation would end well. It was only through the direct and nimble intervention of the neutral Swiss diplomatic representative that disaster was averted. German officials conceded that fatigue duties outside as well as inside the camp would not be considered compulsory labour, while Ottawa acknowledged that all internees who undertook the duties would be paid more than double the standard daily rate – a full fifty cents. With these concessions, the majority returned to their basic work schedule. But the essential dispute remained – namely, they were civilians with natural rights that could not be ignored.[37]

The disturbances in the late fall of 1917 profoundly affected relations between the commandant and troops. Guards were criticized for insubordination and the camp commander was reproached for his high-handedness and ineffectiveness, having shown that he was incapable of keeping the rebelliousness of the prisoners in check. In view of these accusations and failings, the internment director was inclined to relieve Date of his command. Instead, an inquiry was held that eventually led to his exoneration.[38] Nevertheless, a shake-up occurred, with several officers critical of Date's command dismissed while others resigned, having received no satisfaction regarding their grievances.

The lingering resentments ensured that administering Kapuskasing in 1918 would remain a challenge. Several issues compounded the difficulties. Work was being scaled back in response to the difficulty of managing the prisoners, resulting in the discontinuance of prisoner wages. As the wages were used to purchase canteen items (tobacco and sugar), this decision only added to the internees' frustrations and confrontational demeanour. In addition, prisoners working near the railway encountered recently paroled internees, which underscored the unfairness of their continuing incarceration. Then there was the increased cost of covering basic fatigue duties, which unexpectedly added to the camp's expenses. All these raised questions about the future of Kapuskasing. Internment would have to be adjusted if it were to continue to be viable.

Since Kapuskasing's finances had become a pressing issue, a provisional solution was to release some of the prisoners, thereby reducing costs. A precedent already existed for this. Aliens of enemy origin, interned as prisoners because they were unemployed, had been paroled to work in industry once the economy improved. But on what grounds could this now be contemplated? The remaining internees were antagonistic, insubordinate, and therefore their parole was problematic. Moreover, public opinion was hostile, especially among returned veterans, who were solidly against any concessions to enemy aliens in general, let alone war prisoners. For veterans, the push was on to have all enemy aliens interned as POWs and used as compulsory labour, not to have those interned released.

The Department of Justice rejected the idea of mass internment and the compulsory labour of aliens of enemy birth in so far as "it would be impossible to find justification in the Hague Convention or in general international usage for [the] industrial conscription of such aliens."[39] In their assessment, however, officials concluded that, despite the public's hostility, some prisoners could prudently be released if they were properly screened for attitude and their whereabouts and activity monitored. As for those prisoners considered "undesirable" – having demonstrated a visceral dislike of authority and, thus, providing evidence of their enemy sympathies – it was felt they should remain behind barbed wire until a decision was made regarding their future.[40] Diplomatic negotiations regarding the fate of different categories of prisoners were ongoing, and the idea of deporting this residual group was clearly on the minds of the authorities.[41] Thus, a distinction between the acceptable and the "undesirable" enemy alien prisoner was formally introduced, giving shape to a new phase in the internment saga.

Major General Otter instructed Lieutenant Colonel Date and other commanders at the remaining camps to compile lists under Order-in-Council PC 158 (23 January 1918), identifying those who were suitable for possible release and those who were to remain interned until a final decision was made.[42] Soon thereafter and throughout 1918, based on this difference, small groups from Kapuskasing were paroled locally to railway companies. Others were sent to New Brunswick and Nova Scotia, where they also worked on the railways. Those who proved unsatisfactory while there, either in terms of performance or outlook, were returned to Kapuskasing, where, under the watchful guise of Lieutenant Colonel Date, they would await their fate.

With the armistice, the disposition of the internees in Canada became a matter of growing public debate. Within a broader discussion about immigration and the future of aliens of enemy origin, the Canadian public clamoured for the removal of the 2,222 prisoners remaining in the camps. But this was a sentiment that was also motivated, in part, by the fear of political and labour unrest in the country, which enemy aliens were accused of fomenting. Indeed, public sentiment became ever more pronounced regarding the fate of the prisoners, especially with the arrest and internment of enemy alien participants in the May–June 1919 Winnipeg General Strike.[43] The charged atmosphere of labour unrest served to accelerate the calls for deportation.

In reply to inquiries about the presence of undesirables at Kapuskasing, Date reported that, of the 1,007 prisoners there, forty were either labour activists or political militants. An additional 195 relocated from Amherst, Nova Scotia, wore red ribbons when they entered the camp at the time of their transfer – an indication of their disloyalty, it was claimed. Another ninety-five proved troublesome during internment. Sensing there was an appetite for the removal of all of them, Date proffered that, "being a loafing, good for nothing lot, the sooner the country [was] rid of them the better."[44] By order of the Department of Justice, the first batch of

872 prisoners from the three remaining camps – Amherst, Kapuskasing, and Vernon (BC) – was assembled at Quebec City and, on 25 July 1919, mustered onto a ship bound for Rotterdam. Among them were 105 internees from Kapuskasing. Having suffered psychological breakdowns during their internment, another twenty-two prisoners deemed insane (out of fifty-four being held at various asylums) were also included for deportation – part of the general effort to purge the unwanted from the country.

The prospect of further deportations prompted a spate of last-minute personal and legal appeals. Acting on behalf of some internees who had been involved in the Winnipeg General Strike and sent to Kapuskasing, solicitors appealed for due process, but to no avail. Other internees requested clemency with a promise to be law-abiding or, more simply, pleaded for justice, citing that their offence "consisted solely in being of [enemy alien] nationality, regardless of what [they] had once meant to Canada."[45] Then there were those who did not care whether they were allowed to stay or were deported. They simply wanted out.

Canadian authorities would oblige by organizing for transport most of the remaining prisoners – 886 in total – including the last of the insane. On 4 September and 27 October 1919, they boarded ships bound for Europe with a young Captain Kirkconnell in charge of one of the transports. The escorts for each ship were issued one thousand rounds of ammunition in case of trouble. It was unnecessary. Released on the docks of Rotterdam, prisoners were described as "blithe and carefree," wishing their captors a bon voyage – but not before a few shared with them the prediction that they would return to Canada one day to spread the creed of socialism.[46]

Kapuskasing officially closed on 24 February 1920 after the last few internees were paroled. The camp buildings, in the meantime, had been sold to the dominion Department of Agriculture. As for the future of the experimental farm, it was undecided. The first set of colonists – returned soldiers – did not take kindly to the new settlement, having overwintered at the site in 1918–19. An early frost had destroyed the crops, and the cold weather was severe. By all accounts, the experimental farm colony was a disaster. Nonetheless, it was seen as an important step in promoting the potential of Ontario's northland. A template and infrastructure were in place. All that was needed, according to the plan's supporters, was the right type of settler.

Without detracting from what had been accomplished – and it was significant – the real importance of Kapuskasing lay in its deeper meaning. Kapuskasing was a place where civilians designated as POWs were forced to work under armed guard, and, once there, isolated and forgotten, they endured primitive and harsh conditions. It was also a place where some, deemed undesirable, were held until deported. More to the point, Kapuskasing was a place of moral, physical, and psychological danger, where indifference, suspicion, and malice came together to shape the experiences of those interned and those tasked with overseeing their internment. Underlying much of this was the predicament of immigrants originating from distant lands now at war with Canada. There was a tangible sense that the internees did not belong and therefore were owed nothing, their treatment being a function of their peripheral status within the Canadian nation.

At the outset, it would have been inconceivable to them that internment would be their fate.[47] As immigrants, they had made Canada their home. The affairs of the old country were of less importance than getting on with their lives in the new. Yet, for the government, this was immaterial in view of the practical question of what to do with the mass of destitute enemy aliens thrust onto the unemployment rolls. The war measures that followed offered a radical but useful solution: unemployed enemy aliens could be interned as war prisoners and put to work. Still, they were civilians, a fact that presented a challenge to government. Nonetheless, in the context of the conflict, it was precisely the ambiguousness of their status as civilian prisoners that served to justify the practice of compulsory labour.

Unsurprisingly, a policy that determined who these enemy aliens were said to be would shape the Kapuskasing experience. As outsiders without rights, they would be subject to hard, manual labour; as war prisoners, they would be placed under watch and threatened with violence; as enemies, they would be despised and treated with contempt. Many accepted their fate. Some resisted. The majority, however, simply felt a profound sense of betrayal. To be sure, what occurred at Kapuskasing happened elsewhere, being the logical consequence of a policy that disavowed the alien of enemy origin. Nevertheless, Kapuskasing was singled out as a place where ambitions could be realized – notably, opening Ontario's vast north to colonization. In this regard, the interned enemy alien would be used as a resource. But the scale and scope of the operation gave the narrative of Kapuskasing a tempo of its own.

Under both a constantly expanding plan of operations and overseers who were focused on efficiently completing the job at hand, the prisoners were constantly forced to do more. The military guard and the imperious nature of command ensured their compliance. Yet the achievements of Kapuskasing were less a result of the military nature of the operation than of the mercenary notion that nothing was owed to a people who had no claim on the country. So deeply and widely accepted was this idea that there was little concern regarding how these people were to be used and treated. Consequently, what occurred in the camp was seen as legitimate and proper, absolving officials of any responsibility, while giving licence to those who looked to profit from the misfortune of innocents and to martinets who found nothing wrong with exercising their prejudices.

Forcibly putting jobless and indigent enemy aliens to work, Kapuskasing was the epitome of opportunism. But this opportunism did not end when, in response to industrial demand, the camp was nearly emptied of its inmates. The existence of war measures meant that internment might still be of use. Obstreperous prisoners who could not be released had to be dealt with, as did labour activists and progressives (seen to be no less troublesome) whom the government sought to expel. As a result, Kapuskasing, from mid-1917 until the signing of the peace, provided for their detention and deportation as undesirables. In this, Kapuskasing distinguished itself, but only to the extent that it was an acknowledgment of the seminal belief that there was no place in Canada for such people.

Built around the promise of agriculture, the experiment of Kapuskasing ended with mixed results. Captain Watson Kirkconnell, a participant and witness to this experiment, expressed his disappointment that returned soldier-settlers had been unable to make good on the opportunity presented to them. He believed, however, that a hardier, more determined and resilient group of internees would have succeeded where they had not.[48] Yet, what he failed to appreciate (if only because they were thought to be of no importance) was that he witnessed just such a group – those migrants who had been brought to Ontario's northland as prisoners of war. In returning to their families, friends, and communities, and carrying on with their lives in Canada after having been released from their internment, they demonstrated their mettle. In their ordinariness, they prevailed over the extraordinary, and in the process, they proved that they belonged.

EPILOGUE

First World War Internment in Canada and Historical Memory

Acknowledging and Remembering the Past

On 22 September 1988, the Right Honourable Brian Mulroney, prime minister of Canada, rose in the House of Commons to issue an apology to Canadians of Japanese origin for the wrongful internment of their community during the Second World War. The prime minister stated in part on that occasion that Canadians could not change history but that, as a nation, they needed to demonstrate courage to face the past. He spoke in imperatives, declaring that an apology was necessary "to put things right with the surviving members – with their children, and ours so that they can walk together in this country, burdened by neither the wrongs nor the grievances of previous generations."[1] With noble and generous words, the prime minister described Canada as a place where people could come together in trust and harmony with an abiding respect for each other's cultures and histories. But he also acknowledged that, in great measure, the nation's ability to face the challenges of tomorrow and the moral choices that Canadians made today depended on whether it was prepared to understand and redress the mistakes of the past.

In those few well-chosen words, the prime minister set before the nation the practical importance of passing moral judgment on past injustices. Moral judgments have implications for actions and, thus, for the current and future conduct of human affairs. The value of recognizing a historical wrong lies in the meaning it has for the recognition of other potentially unjust events. Our condemnation of a historical injustice conditions our response to current injustices. It also reinforces a tradition that allows us to avoid actions that would imperil both our moral worth and our identity as a people committed to justice. As a nation, Canada must address historical injustices because it is in this way that Canadians become open to those ideas and values that we as a democratic people profess to use in addressing our current actions.

However, there are other imperatives behind our need to acknowledge historical wrongs. Historical memory enables us to speak intelligently about the circumstances that have affected people and wounded their dignity. By acknowledging the suffering and pain of the past, by making amends through the process of restoring history, we signal to those communities against whom an injustice was committed that reconciliation is possible. We convey to them that they have not only worth but also a place in the story that is Canada. We commit to them that what occurred will not be forgotten.

Historical memory also enables us to identify those situations that manifest moral ambivalence. By acknowledging and accepting that what happened was real, in doing our best to recover the history that was lost, we protect ourselves from the confusion fomented by those who, in the absence of facts, would lead us to believe in alternative narratives about the past. We avoid being ensnared in myths that shelter and even exempt us from accepting our responsibility to hear and ascertain what went wrong and why an injustice occurred.

It is frequently argued that judging past wrongs is futile. This, however, misses the point of history and moral judgment. That we cannot change history is obvious. The issue is to confront and learn from it because it tells us something about who we are. As for those who would dismiss the lessons of history, our frustration and disappointment lie not in the contempt they display for the process of discovery; rather, it lies in losing the opportunity to learn how to avoid repeating those mistakes.

This, of course, is not to suggest that historical memory is prescriptive, or that the lessons of history lead inexorably to a higher consciousness. Far from it. The value of revealing and examining the past is to alert those faced with moral choices to the myriad possibilities presented by political choices both now and in the future. Actions and decisions must be weighed carefully, and, in navigating our choices, historical memory helps guide us.

Remembering allows us to grapple with the seemingly random nature of history, comprised, as it is, of events that, at first glance, appear puzzling and even unintelligible. History is a complex and layered affair. Only a complete recollection of things past can assist us in our understanding of it. However, concealing an event or dismissing it as insignificant damages historical memory. History then becomes an even greater catalogue of disconnected and incoherent events, void of meaning or relevance.

The importance of historical memory is that it helps frame and support the identities of communities and individuals, anchoring and lending meaning to their existence. If historical memory is trivialized or derided as irrelevant, an assault on identity occurs. Not only is the importance of what happened minimized, but responsibility is shifted away from those liable for it. Accordingly, the original offenders are absolved and those who would create what they see as a more palatable history are given licence to do so. Only through remembrance are we able to reject the prevaricating and dissembling accounts that are substituted for what actually occurred. Only through historical memory can communities and individuals maintain their cultural and moral worth within a world of conjecture and recrimination, while dispelling arguments that rely on historical and moral relativism to diminish an injustice.

Without a commitment to restoring the past, without remembering, we are left in the dark about the nature of an injustice. This undermines not only our belief in justice but also our understanding that rights matter, the rule of law matters, and, more profoundly, people matter. Only by hearing their story are we able to comprehend more fully what happened to them and, in doing so, to understand the nature of the injustice they suffered. Only by placing them at the centre of the narrative – by ensuring that their experiences are described and explained – can justice be restored. Moreover, by profiling their experience we gain a greater appreciation of what should be our guiding values. By remembering, we gain clarity about who we are as a nation and how we must conduct ourselves in the future.

In a campaign for redress, no amount of compensation will ever serve as adequate restitution for a historical wrong, especially one that deprived individuals of their basic human rights. It is for this reason that redress can only be symbolic. However, in its symbolism, redress – according to Prime Minister Mulroney's address to the House of Commons – must go beyond "laws and words." A cornerstone of redress must be a commitment to restore history, to retell past events in their entirety as a demonstration of society's undertaking to acknowledge that a wrong once occurred. Redress, however, must also preserve the integrity and dignity of a people's identity by making clear that there can be no indifference to injustice, even if it was the government that acted unjustly. This, of course, places a special obligation on the government not only to lead in the effort to acknowledge the wrongdoing but also to put into place protections for future generations.

The settlement reached between the government of Canada and the Japanese Canadian community was successfully concluded because the apology was unequivocal and, symbolically, met the criteria of responsibility. The apology was neither taken nor meant to be an act of contrition or atonement because neither was being sought. The personal human toll, the psychological turbulence, and the material losses suffered by the Japanese Canadian community are part of that experience and can never be fully compensated. What was sought, however, was a sincere expression of good faith: recognition that an injustice had been committed, symbolic restitution so that the nation could move forward, and the introduction of legal safeguards to prevent a recurrence of what had happened.

The imperatives that we learn from Japanese Canadian internment are no less pressing than those we learn from the First World War "enemy alien" experience. During the Great War, Canada interned migrants of so-called enemy origin on the pretext of national security concerns, but this pretext was extended to address routine concerns as well. This was a political choice. It was also a moral choice. At the time, some officials understood the immoral nature of this choice and either opposed the use of internment as unwarranted and unjust or expressed unease about its effects. Still others, including those who were directly affected, simply asked: Was there not an obligation to deal fairly with people who had been encouraged to settle in Canada? Was Canada not their home? History reveals the poignancy of these questions and the moral jeopardy in which the nation was placed.

Today, Canadians are faced with the challenge of learning from this history. Whether they are prepared to face the past is uncertain. It is not encouraging when, for example, Canada's heritage minister, who, responsible for the national parks where internment took place and tourists now travel untroubled on roads forcibly built by innocent migrants, dismisses the wrongdoing as being of no historical value and the public in no need of awareness or education.[2] It is not promising when appeals for respectful recognition and symbolic redress are contemptuously dismissed by a member of Parliament as "claims that go back to the Dark Ages."[3]

It is also unclear to what degree a government can ever commit to the process of redress as a form of reconciliation when officials and politicians cynically characterize it as a scheme motivated by avarice.[4] Only by reclaiming the past can we address the deception, confusion, and malevolence that discredits the injustice that so cruelly affected innocent individuals. Only by remembering can we give voice to the idea that these people mattered and what they experienced was real.

The imperatives that forced the government to examine its obligations and responsibility to the present and the future with regard to Japanese Canadians are no less compelling in this case. The democratic precepts behind the Canadian polity underscore the importance that both the rule of law and the recognition of human rights have for the nation's future. Canada's internment of enemy aliens during the First World War serves as a reminder of the fragile nature of the political foundations of this country. History provides us with lessons that might decrease our likelihood of repeating past mistakes. The importance of this should not be lost on those who aspire to lead the country and are now routinely faced with political and moral choices.

The issue of acknowledging and remembering historical wrongs, a keystone of redress, presents us with a major challenge. Whether we can adequately address this issue will test the country's commitment to rights and justice. The significance of this challenge lies not in its implications for those affected communities but, rather, for the country as a whole and the political foundations upon which it rests. Are Canadians prepared to face the past? Will Canadians understand how the wrong perpetrated against so-called enemy aliens endangered the moral character of the nation and that its legacy continues to exercise a pernicious and corrupting influence?

History, of course, cannot be undone and its effects linger. The experience of internment is an integral part of the historical and collective memory of those affected, of their descendants, and of the communities they represent. That this history may be dismissed or trivialized is unfortunate, constituting an unnecessary burden. If they are not challenged, those who would normalize this injustice will believe that they may do so with impunity. The initial wrong is compounded as a result, and we are left to stumble in the dark, puzzled by how such indifference accords with the narrative of Canada as a just nation. Acknowledgment and remembrance can help us to reconcile the seemingly irreconcilable – to overcome the miasma.

Within this process of reconciliation lies an opportunity to grow. If we can overcome our prejudices and move towards discovering what we might yet become, then this will be a true measure of the political maturity of the Canadian people and an uncompromising expression of solidarity with the future. Discovery, however, can only begin by acknowledging and embracing the story of internment, by sharing a commitment to remember, and, in the effort to understand, by creating a place that we may all call home.

NOTES

Introduction

1 For a detailed account of the John Kondro case, see Bohdan S. Kordan and Peter Melnycky, eds, *In the Shadow of the Rockies: Diary of the Castle Mountain Internment Camp, 1915–1917* (Edmonton, CIUS Press, 1991), 6.

2 On the role of migrant workers and their struggles during this formative period in Canada's economic and social history, see Donald Avery, *"Dangerous Foreigners": European Immigrant Workers and Labour Radicalism in Canada, 1896–1932* (Toronto: McClelland and Stewart, 1979).

3 On immigration policy goals and process in the lead up to the war, see Triadafilos Triadafilopolous, "Building Walls, Bounding Nations: Migration and Exclusion in Canada and Germany, 1870-1939," *Journal of Historical Sociology* 17, no. 4 (2004): 396–400.

4 See the discussion in Howard Palmer, *Patterns of Prejudice: A History of Nativism in Alberta* (Toronto: McClelland and Stewart, 1982), chap. 1.

5 On the war convention and the rights of POWs and civilian prisoners, see Richard Speed, *Prisoner, Diplomats, and the Great War: A Study in the Diplomacy of Captivity* (New York: Greenwood, 1990).

6 The War Measures Act granted the executive branch of government wide powers to regulate the activities of enemy aliens. It also conferred on the government the power to arrest and intern based on perceived security needs in the context of war. This was largely discretionary. Since espionage and sabotage were felt to be rooted in the social-cultural make-up of the enemy, it was felt that enemy aliens could be dealt with and treated as POWs. The power to intern an enemy alien as a war prisoner was legally challenged in Britain but soon rejected by the courts (*R. v. Superintendent of Vine Street Police Station; Ex Parte Liebmann*). This court decision was used by Canadian authorities to justify the government's authority to intern. See Peter McDermott, "Internment during the Great War – A Challenge to the Rule of Law," *UNSW Law Journal*, 282, no. 2 (2005): 342–3.

7 Jacob Kondro to Brigadier General E. Cruikshank, 8 February 1916, file: 2, vol. 4721, RG 24, Library and Archives Canada (hereafter LAC).

8 Nira Yuval-Davis makes an analytical distinction around the notion of belonging as either an emotional attachment or a political process. The latter

entails the maintenance of boundaries – a predominate concern of Anglo-Canadian society at the turn of the century. On the politics of belonging, see Nira Yuval-Davis, "Borders, Boundaries and the Politics of Belonging," in *Ethnicity, Nationalism and Minority Rights*, ed. Stephen May, Tariq Modood, and Judith Squires (Cambridge: Cambridge University Press, 2004).

9 See Ninette Kelley and Michael Trebilcock, *The Making of the Mosaic: A History of Canadian Immigration Policy* (Toronto: University of Toronto Press, 1998), chap. 4.

10 The most authoritative writer on the imperial idea as it manifests itself in Canada is Carl Berger, *The Sense of Power: Studies in the Ideas of Canadian Imperialism* (Toronto: University of Toronto Press, 1970).

11 See James R. Carruthers, "The Great War and Canada's Enemy Alien Policy," *Queen's Law Journal* 4 (1978): 43–110.

12 The discretionary interpretation of the security regulations naturally led to uneven enforcement. Illegal arrests occurred as a result, including that of naturalized citizens. On arbitrary enforcement, see Mary Chaktsiris, "Identifying the Enemy in First World War Canada: The Historiography and Bureaucracy of Enemy Alien Internment and Registration," *Canadian Military History* 28, no. 2 (2019): 15–22.

13 Other states would resort to the internment of civilians but not because they were unemployed. See Stefan Manz, Panikos Panayi, and Matthew Stibbe, "Introduction," in *Internment during the First World War: A Mass Global Phenomenon*, ed. Stefan Manz, Panikos Panayi, and Matthew Stibbe (London: Routledge, 2019), 6–7.

14 Because "the principle of self-preservation must justify belligerents in refusing to furnish each other with resources which increase their means of offence and defence," legal scholars – a minority at the time – maintained that enemy aliens could be interned as POWs. But tradition also held that such individuals were to be accorded tolerance and respect while interned, intimating that there was a distinction to be made between POWs and interned civilian enemy aliens. As a result, the description "civilian POW" would identify their status. The difficulty was the lack of specificity in international law on the rights of civilians as prisoners. On captive civilian enemy aliens and lack of clarity in international law, see Speed, *Prisoner, Diplomats, and the Great War*, 142–3.

15 See Jonathan Swainger, "Erroneous and Detestable: Seditious Language and the Great War in Western Canada," in *Canadian State Trials*, vol. 4, *Security, Dissent, and the Limits of Toleration in War and Peace, 1914–1939*, ed. Barry Wright, Eric Tucker, and Susan Binnie (Toronto: University of Toronto Press, 2015).

16 This said nothing about the basic question of the legality of the internment of enemy aliens. Where their detention was challenged, the courts declined to enquire about the validity of internment because of the existing state of emergency. See Peter McDermott, "Enemy Aliens in the First World War:

Legal and Constitutional Issues," in Wright, Tucker, Binnie, eds., *Canadian State Trials* 4: 77–80.

17 As a dominion, Canada did not possess full sovereignty over its external affairs, and Canadian interests were represented by London. As a result, there was little occasion for Canada to engage diplomatically with other foreign powers. The internment issue proved the exception, with a robust exchange taking place over an extended period between Canada and Germany via the United Kingdom, with neutral states acting as liaisons. For an analysis and discussion of Canada's early external affairs in an imperial context, see George P. de T. Glazebrook, *A History of Canadian External Relations* (Toronto: McClelland and Stewart, 1966), vol. 2, chap. 12.

18 On the connection between the global and local dimensions of internment, see Manz, Panayi, and Stibbe, *Internment during the First World War.*

19 Caroline Elkins argues that violence was an integral part of British imperial rule. From this perspective, internment is seen as a form of brutal authority introduced on the frontier as part of the "missionizing" spirit of British civilization, imposing the global imperative of imperial rule within a local context. See Caroline Elkins, *Legacy of Violence: A History of the British Empire* (New York: Vintage, 2023).

20 Prisoners were variously categorized as military prisoners, civilian prisoners, and/or political prisoners. These categories were used interchangeably to justify differential treatment. "Despite the fact that the different legal frameworks influencing the life of prisoners were different and distinct, it is clear that in many cases the interning power used more than one framework vs-a-vis a particular group of prisoners to legitimate its actions." See Iris Rachaminov and Rotem Kowner, "Military, Civilian and Political Internments: Examining Great War Internments Together," in *Out of Line, Out of Place: A Global and Local History of World War I Internments*, ed. Rotem Kowner and Iris Rachaminov (Ithaca, NY: Cornell University Press, 2022), 9.

21 Despite the pressure exerted on government for greater control of the enemy alien, the government was careful not to unnecessarily aggravate the security situation for fear of disrupting the economy and contributing to social strife. This argument is made by Brock Millman, *Polarity, Patriotism, and Dissent in Great War Canada, 1914–1919* (Toronto: University of Toronto Press, 2016).

22 See Jeffrey Keshen, *Propaganda and Censorship during Canada's Great War* (Edmonton: University of Alberta Press, 1996).

23 Wartime mobilization of the civilian population augmented the threat perception of the enemy alien, triggering a response at the personal level: "Traditionally, the army was the sole legal repository of violence in war. However, mass conscription, the popular press, and the growth of nationalism meant in 1914 many civilians felt personally called to act against the perceived threat to their nation – every citizen was called upon to stop spies

and saboteurs." See Heather Jones, *Violence against Prisoners of War in the First World War* (Cambridge: Cambridge University Press, 2011), 39.

24 See Donald Avery, "Ethnic and Class Relations in Western Canada during the First World War: A Case Study of European Immigrants and Anglo-Canadian Nativism," in *Canada and the First World War*, ed. D. Mackenzie (Toronto: University of Toronto Press, 2018); and Donald Avery, "Ethnic and Class Tensions in Canada, 1918–20: Anglo-Canadians and the Alien Worker," in *Loyalties in Conflict: Ukrainians in Canada during the Great War*, ed. Francis Swyripa and John Herd Thompson (Edmonton: CIUS Press, 1983).

25 For a discussion of the militarization of identity and the gendering of conflict, see Sonja Levsen, "Masculinities," in *International Encyclopedia of the First World War*, ed. Ute Daniel, Peter Gatrell, Oliver Janz, Heather Jones, Jennifer Keene, Alan Kramer, and Bill Nasson (issued by Freie Universität Berlin, Berlin 2015-01-07), DOI: 10.15463/ie1418.10531.

26 On the important role that the press has played in instigating majority hostility to "outgroups" during wartime, see Panikos Panayi, "Dominant Societies and Minorities in the Two World Wars," in *Minorities in Wartime: National and Racial Groupings in Europe, North America, and Australia during the Two World Wars*, ed. Panikos Panayi (Oxford: Berg, 1993), 12–14. For a reading of the press' part in creating local anti-German resentments in Canada, see Peter Moogk, "Uncovering the Enemy Within: British Columbians and the German Menace," *BC Studies* 182 (Summer 2014): 73–112; and William J. Campbell, "'We Germans ... Are British Subjects'": The First World War and the Curious Case of Berlin, Ontario, Canada," *Canadian Military History* 21, no. 2 (2015): 45–57.

27 During the war, but especially in the latter stages of the conflict as well as in its aftermath, the government employed security measures, including internment, against labour and political activists who were deemed dangerous. See Gregory Kealey, "State Repression of Labour and the Left in Canada, 1914–1920," *Canadian Historical Review* 73, no. 3 (September 1992): 281–314; and Avery, *"Dangerous Foreigners,"* chap. 3. Placed in the camps, they were to be deported along with those who remained interned and were considered "undesirable." On internment and deportation, see Barbara Roberts, *Whence They Came: Deportation from Canada, 1900–1935* (Ottawa: University of Ottawa Press, 1988), chaps 2 and 3.

28 By way of comparison, for a study of the campaign against enemy aliens in Australia and the interactive role between the public, press, and government, see Gerhard Fischer, "Fighting the War at Home: The Campaign against Enemy Aliens in Australia during the First World War," in Panayi, *Minorities in Wartime*, 263–86.

29 See John Herd Thompson, *The Harvests of War: The Prairie West, 1914–1918* (Toronto: McClelland and Stewart, 1978); Robert Rutherdale, *Hometown Horizons: Local Responses to Canada's Great War* (Vancouver: UBC Press, 2004); Nathan Smith, "Fighting the Alien Problem in a British Country: Returned

Soldiers and Anti-Alien Activism in Wartime Canada, 1916–19," in *Other Combatants, Other Fronts: Competing Histories of the First World War*, ed. James E. Kitchen, Alisa Miller, and Laura Rowe (Newcastle: Cambridge Scholars Publishing, 2011); and Mary Chaktsiris, "The Enemy at Home: Defining Enemy Aliens in Ontario during the Great War," in *The Great War from Memory to History*, ed. Kellen Kurschinski, Steve Martin, Alicia Robinet, Matt Symes, and Jonathan Vance (Waterloo: Wilfrid Laurier University Press, 2015).

30 Captain Watson Kirkconnell published two stories of his experience as an officer at the Kapuskasing camp shortly after demobilization. See Watson Kirkconnell, "Kapuskasing: A Historical Sketch," *Bulletin of the Departments of History and Political and Economic Science in Queen's University* 38 (January 1921): 264–78; and Watson Kirkconnell, "When We First Locked Up Fritz: The First Authentic Story of Our Internment Camps," *Maclean's*, 1 September 1920.

A few descriptions of camp life were also left by prisoners, not least of which was an account by Leon Trotsky, who, travelling between New York and Europe in 1917, was seized on the high seas and interned at Amherst, Nova Scotia. See Leon Trotsky, *My Life* (New York: Charles Scribners and Sons, 1930), chap. 23. The memoir of Adolph Hundt was reproduced by Dominique Villeneuve in *Heritage by Default, 1914–1920* (Kapuskasing: n.p., 2014). The reminiscence of John Boychuk was reworked as a graphic novel by Kassandra Luciuk, *Enemy Alien: A True Story of Life behind Barbed Wire* (Toronto: Between the Lines, 2020), while several oral accounts by prisoners at the Fort Henry internment camp were transcribed and reproduced in Lubomyr Luciuk, *Internment Operations: The Role of Old Fort Henry in World War I* (Kingston: Delta, 1980). See also P. Yasnowsky, "Internment," in *Land of Pain, Land of Promise: First Person Accounts of Ukrainian Pioneers, 1890–1914*, ed. Harry Piniuta (Saskatoon: Western Producer Prairie Books, 1978).

31 The surreal nature of First World War internment in Canada's national parks was especially poignant: "[In building the parks] the internees had known only exhaustion, suffering, fear, and desolation. They also learned about a darker side of Canadian life and their place on the margins of Canadian society. The cruellest blow was being confined in what were being widely promoted as Canada's national playgrounds. For several years thereafter 'These are your parks … Come and enjoy them' would haunt many immigrants who, despite their wartime treatment, had decided to make Canada their home." See Bill Waiser, *Park Prisoners: The Untold Story of Western Canada's National Parks, 1915–1946* (Saskatoon/Calgary: Fifth House, 1995), 47.

32 Nira Yuval-Davis, "Belonging and the Politics of Belonging," *Patterns of Prejudice* 40, no. 3 (2006): 197–214; and John Crowley, "The Politics of Belonging: Some Theoretical Considerations," in *The Politics of Belonging: Migrants and Minorities in Contemporary Europe*, ed. Adrian Favell and Andrew Geddes (Aldershot, UK: Ashgate, 1999).

33 On the myths associated with civilian internment, including the myth of "military necessity," see Matthew Stibbe, *Civilian Internment during the First World War: A European and Global History, 1914–1920* (London: Palgrave, 2020).

34 W. James Booth, *Communities of Memory: On Witness, Identity, and Justice* (Ithaca, NY: Cornell University Press, 2006); Janna Thompson, "Apology, Historical Obligations and the Ethics of Memory," *Memory Studies* 2, no. 2 (2009): 195–210; and Bohdan S. Kordan, *First World War Internment in Canada: Policy, Practice and Political Ethics* (Saskatoon: Heritage Press, 2023).

Chapter One

A variant of this text was co-authored with James Farney and originally published as James Farney and Bohdan S. Kordan, "The Predicament of Belonging: The Status of Enemy Aliens in Canada, 1914," *Journal of Canadian Studies* 39, no. 1 (2005): 74–89

1 Standard works on the treatment of immigrants in Canada prior to and during the First World War include, among others, D. Avery, *Reluctant Host: Canada's Response to Immigrant Workers, 1896–1994* (Toronto: McClelland and Stewart, 1995); and H. Palmer, *Patterns of Prejudice: A History of Nativism in Alberta* (Toronto: McClelland and Stewart, 1982).

2 Before the twentieth century, mass internment of civilians was unforeseen, and, therefore, the laws of land war remained silent (except in special circumstances) with respect to the treatment of civilian prisoners of war. The necessity of mass conscription during the Great War, however, prompted a preliminary response. By way of accommodation and reciprocity, the principle arrived at maintained that civilians of enemy origin who were interned as non-combatants were to be subject to an even higher standard of conduct and treatment than that which the various war conventions outlined for military prisoners. See R. Speed, *Prisoners, Diplomats, and the Great War: A Study in the Diplomacy of Captivity* (New York: Greenwood, 1990), 142–4.

3 Ibid., 155–66.

4 Overall, Britain retained de jure control through the governor general and the Judicial Committee of the Privy Council, but the autonomy of Canadian authorities in fact depended on the division of labour between Britain and Canada based on the separation of Canadian sovereignty into its internal and external aspects. Canadian governments insisted that their responsibility to the Canadian Parliament implied that it was the government of Canada, and not the government of Britain, that should be charged with authority in domestic Canadian affairs. As for external authority, despite the transfer of certain aspects of external sovereignty (notably trade and local defence) to Canada, in 1914, the security of the empire remained the preserve of the British government. Not until the 1931 Statute of Westminster would Great Britain assign to Canada most of the roles associated with ex-

ternal sovereignty. Because of external sovereignty's indeterminate definition, Canada's exact external powers before the First World War were more often a matter of political understanding than of legal precedent. See A.B. Keith, *The Sovereignty of the British Dominions* (London: St Martins, 1929), 207–10; and R.M. Dawson, *The Development of Dominion Status, 1900–1936* (London: Oxford University Press, 1937), 5–7.

5 The concept of subjectship is taken from J. Kettner, *The Development of American Citizenship, 1608–1870* (Chapel Hill: University of North Carolina Press, 1978), 3–8.

6 D.E. Smith, *The Republican Option in Canada: Past and Present* (Toronto: University of Toronto Press, 1999), 175.

7 Keith, *Sovereignty of the British Dominions*, 62–3.

8 The 1881 Naturalization and Aliens Act brought Canadian law into agreement with the original 1870 Naturalization Act. Since the 1906 act fit into the same framework, there were no substantial differences between them. See C. Parry, *Nationality and Citizenship Laws of the Commonwealth and the Republic of Ireland* (London: Stevens and Sons, 1957), 1:442.

9 G.T. Tamaki, "The Law Relating to Nationality in Canada" (LLM thesis, University of Toronto, 1944), 126.

10 If, for example, a Canadian citizen who was not a British subject moved to the United Kingdom, then that individual was classed as an alien. The result was that, in a polity based on personal relationships with the Crown, those who could relate to the Crown in both its internal and external aspects had a fuller relationship with it than did those who could only relate to one of its aspects. However, since Canada held the internal aspects of sovereignty and Great Britain held the external aspects, immigrants who were naturalized Canadian citizens only (and not British subjects) had no relation with the latter.

11 Tamaki, "Law Relating to Nationality in Canada," 76.

12 C. Berger, *The Sense of Power: Studies in the Idea of Canadian Imperialism, 1867–1914* (Toronto: University of Toronto Press, 1970), 6. The one weakness in Berger's discussion is that he sometimes conflates nationalists with imperialists. His discussion of the background of the two movements is, however, unsurpassed. For a clear distinction between nationalist and imperialist, see A.G. Dewey, *The Dominions and Diplomacy: The Canadian Contribution* (London: Longman, 1929), 4–18.

13 Berger, *Sense of Power*, 78, 139.

14 Ibid., 145.

15 Douglas Cole notes that an important "chord which ran through the thought of all imperialists was a concern with ethnic traits and their own ethnicity." "[They] were imperialists in large measure," he argued," because they were acutely aware of ethnic ties and ethnic differentiation." See Douglas Cole, "Canada's 'Nationalistic' Imperialists," *Journal of Canadian Studies*, 5, no. 3 (1970): 45.

16 Kettner, *Development of American Citizenship,* 20.
17 Ibid., 18–19.
18 Ibid., 20.
19 The institutional Crown, in Britain as in Canada, is seen to absorb the role of personal kingship. See D.E. Smith, *The Invisible Crown: The First Principle of Canadian Government* (Toronto: University of Toronto Press, 1995), 21.
20 Similarly, it was felt that naturalized British subjects who owed allegiance to another Crown could not be fully trusted. As a result, in some cases, their naturalization was revoked to ensure that they reverted to the status of enemy aliens.
21 Kettner, *Development of American Citizenship,* 18–19. In the case of Germany, the idea of continuing service based on pre-existing political loyalty derived from the German law on nationality – the Delbruck Act – which stated: "It is true that we recognize that there are cases where a German citizen abroad may have an interest in acquiring side by side with his old nationality a new nationality, the possession of which would still allow him to usefully represent the interests of his old fatherland."
22 To be sure, war brought with it legal changes that made it more difficult for all residents of Canada – subjects, citizens, and aliens alike – to enjoy the privileges gained from being linked to the Crown. However, the Defence of the Realm Act, 1914, and its Canadian equivalent, the War Measures Act, 1914, by militarizing the relationship between individuals and the polity, made the status of immigrants doubly vulnerable. Being classified as persons outside the Canadian polity, enemy aliens, because of their status as foreign subjects, would not only be treated as individuals without rights but would also be subject to military law – despite being civilians. See J.R. Carruthers, "The Great War and Canada's Enemy Alien Policy," *Queen's Law Journal* 4 (1978): 54.
23 J. Schull, *Laurier: The First Canadian* (Toronto: Macmillan, 1965), 79.
24 D. Owram, *Promise of Eden: The Canadian Expansionist Movement and the Idea of the West, 1856–1900* (Toronto: University of Toronto Press, 1980), 126.
25 J.C. Lehr, "Government Perceptions of Ukrainian Immigrants to Western Canada, 1896–1902." *Canadian Ethnic Studies* 19 (1987): 9.
26 J.S. Woodsworth, *Strangers within Our Gates* (Toronto: Methodist Church, 1909), 134–5.
27 While some immigrants from Austria-Hungary were able to serve in the Canadian Expeditionary Force – many with distinction – those who wished to enlist had to conceal their national origin. Among Ukrainians, for example, this meant claiming that they had been born in the Russian Empire when, in fact, they had been born in Austria-Hungary. Those whom the authorities discovered in this ruse were often interned as enemy aliens despite their declarations of loyalty to Canada. See L. Luciuk, *In Fear of the Barbed Wire Fence: Canada's First National Internment Operations and the Ukrainian Canadians* (Kingston, ON: Kashtan Press, 2001), 98–100.

28 Canada, Royal Proclamation. *Extra Canada Gazette* 48, no. 7 (5 August 1914): 530–1.
29 Ibid., 10 (5 September 1914): 767.
30 Ibid., 775.

Chapter Two

A variant of this text was originally published as Bohdan S. Kordan, "They Will Be Dangerous: Security and the Control of Enemy Aliens in Canada, 1914," in *Canadian State Trials*, vol. 4, *Security, Dissent and the Limits of Toleration in War and Peace, 1914–1939*, ed. Barry Wright, Eric Tucker, and Susan Binnie (Toronto: University of Toronto Press, 2015).

1 See F.M. Greenwood, "The Drafting and Passage of the War Measures Act in 1914 and 1927: Object Lessons in the Need for Vigilance," in *Canadian Perspectives on Law and Society: Issues in Legal History*, ed. W. Pue and B. Wright (Ottawa: Carleton University Press 1988); and P. Peppin, "Emergency Legislation and Rights in Canada: The War Measures Act and Civil Liberties," *Queen's Law Journal* 18, no. 1 (1993): 129–90.

2 "I do hereby declare that I am a German (an Austro-Hungarian) subject; I now, in consideration of my exemption from detention as a subject of Germany (Austria-Hungary), do hereby undertake and promise that I will report to such officials and upon such terms as the Canadian authorities may from time to time prescribe; that I will carefully observe the laws of the United Kingdom of Great Britain and Ireland and of Canada and such rules as may be especially laid down for my conduct; that I will strictly abstain from taking up arms and from doing any act of hostility towards the Government of this country." Canada, Department of the Secretary of State, *Copies of Proclamations, Orders in Council and Documents Relating to the European War* (Ottawa: Government Print Bureau, 1915), 49–52.

3 Public anxiety centring on the issue of loyalty was largely misplaced, according to the evidence. The chief commissioner of the Dominion Police, A.P. Sherwood, noted from a general reading of police reports that there was no evidence anywhere in the country that enemy aliens were organizing and that the rumours, of which the principal source was the press, were "altogether exaggerated and wholly founded on individual utterances, behind which there is no effective organization." See Lieutenant Colonel A.P. Sherwood, Chief Commissioner of Police, 4 September 1914, reel C-4388, 105989, vol. 191, MG 26 H1(c), Robert Borden Papers, LAC; and Prime Minister Robert Borden, 7 September 1914, reel C-4388, 106024, vol. 191, MG 26 H1(c), Robert Borden Papers, LAC.

4 W.H. Bradley, US Consulate, Montreal, 17 November 1914, file 763.72115/274, State Department Records, United States National Archives (hereafter USNA).

5 Ibid.

6 Reverend M.C. Kinsale, Presbyterian Mission to the Foreigners, Sydney NS, 24 September 1914, file 2165B, vol. 793, RG 6 H3, LAC.

7 Thomas Mulvey, Under Secretary of State, 29 September 1914, file 2165B, vol. 793, RG 6 H3, LAC; and Lieutenant Colonel A.P. Sherwood, Chief Commissioner of Dominion Police, 30 September 1914, file 2165B, vol. 793, RG 6 H3, LAC.

8 Corporal G. Binning, RNWMP detachment, North Portal, Saskatchewan, 18 September 1914, pt. 92–100, no. 170, file 1914, vol. 1770, RG 18, LAC.

9 Officer Commanding 3rd Division, 22 August 1914, file 26-3-12-(2), vol. 4413, RG 4, LAC.

10 W. Homan, Immigration Inspector-in-Charge, Niagara Falls, Ottawa, 26 August 1914, file 884866(2), vol. 603, RG 76, LAC.

11 See, for example, *Manitoba Free Press* (Winnipeg), 14 September 1914.

12 Ibid., 26 August 1914.

13 *Calgary Daily Herald*, 27 August 1914.

14 *Ottawa Evening Journal*, 9 September 1914.

15 *Calgary Daily Herald*, 10 September 1914.

16 Report of Malcolm Reid, Immigration Branch, Vancouver, n.d., file 752149-pt.1, "W.S.D.-2," vol. 486, RG 76, LAC.

17 *Montreal Gazette*, 27 October 1914.

18 Ibid., 24 October 1914.

19 *Manitoba Free Press* (Winnipeg), 24 October 1914.

20 *Montreal Gazette*, 27 October 1914. Members of Montreal's Board of Trade, as organizers of the meeting, solicited support for their position from other municipal boards of trade. They were not to be disappointed, receiving several endorsements. See, for example, F. Morley, Toronto Board of Trade, 31 October 1914, reel C-4388, 106266, MG 26 H1(c), Borden Papers, LAC.

21 Colonel S. Hughes, Minister of Defence and Militia, 18 August 1914, reel C-4235, 21167, Borden Papers, LAC.

22 Sir Thomas Shaughnessy, 26 August 1914, reel C-4388, 105935, Borden Papers, LAC.

23 Sir Robert Borden, Prime Minister of Canada, 27 August 1914, reel C-4388, 105941, Borden Papers, LAC.

24 Meighen was not the only advocate of "a back to the land" movement. The plan made for a public debate that was carried on the pages of the major dailies. See, for instance, *Vancouver Sun*, 27, 28, 30 October, and 2 November. The idea of assisting the unemployed in acquiring plots of land that would help them while alleviating the unemployment problem was endorsed by the mayor and city administration of Calgary and in Regina by the municipal Board of Trade. See *Calgary Daily Herald*, 29 October 1914; and *Edmonton Bulletin*, 25 November 1914.

25 Arthur Meighen, 4 September 1914, reel C-4388, 105995, vol. 191, MG 26 H1(c), Borden Papers, LAC.

26 Sir Robert Borden, 20 October 1914, reel C-4446, 169306, vol. 192, MG 26 H1(c), Borden Papers, LAC.

27 Sir George Perley, Canadian High Commissioner, 22 October 1914, reel C-4388, 106260, vol. 191, MG 26 H1(c), Borden Papers, LAC.

28 L. Harcourt, Secretary, Colonial Office, 26 October 1914, reel C-4388, 106262, vol. 191, MG 26 H1(c), Borden Papers, LAC; and Sir George Perley, 30 October 1914, 106258, vol. 191, MG 26 H1(c), Borden Papers, LAC.

29 Copy of letter: A. Chevalier, Director, Philanthropic Societies of Montreal, 17 September 1914, file 1915-2794, vol. 5299, RG 2, LAC. See also *Montreal Gazette*, 19 October 1914.

30 Sir Robert Borden, 3 October 1914, reel C-4388, 106153-4, vol. 191, MG 26 H1(c), Borden Papers, LAC.

31 W.D. Scott, Superintendent of Immigration, 23 September 1914, file 88486 (3), vol. 603, RG 76, LAC.

32 See *Montreal Gazette*, 28 October 1914.

33 Ibid., 30 October 1914.

34 E. Newcombe, Deputy Minister of Justice, "Registration of Enemy Aliens," 19 November 1914, file 139-59, vol. 191, RG 13 A2, LAC.

35 *Calgary Daily Herald*, 12 November 1914.

36 British Imperial Association (Toronto), 2 November 1914, reel C-4388, 106273, vol. 191, MG 26 H1(c), Robert Borden Papers, LAC.

37 *Calgary Daily Herald*, 3 November 1914.

38 Ibid., 4 November 1914.

39 *Vancouver Sun*, 3 November 1914.

40 Ibid., 28 November 1914.

41 *Daily British Whig* (Kingston), 5 December 1914; *Edmonton Daily Bulletin*, 17 and 25 December 1914.

42 *Manitoba Free Press*, 17 November 1914.

Chapter Three

The following text represents a variant of a combination of published essays. These originally appeared as Bohdan S. Kordan, "First World War Internment in Canada: Enemy Aliens and the Blurring of the Military/Civilian Distinction," *Canadian Military History* 29, 1 (2020): 1–28; and Bohdan S. Kordan, "Internment in Canada during the Great War: Rights, Responsibilities and Diplomacy," in *Internment during the First World War: A Mass Global Phenomenon*, ed. S. Manz, P. Panayi and M. Stibbe (London: Routledge, 2019).

1 Heather Jones, "The Great War: How 1914–18 Changed the Relationship between War and Civilians," *RUSI Journal* 159, no. 4 (2014): 87–9.

2 Annette Becker describes this drawing of civilians into the vortex of war as the "war of fronts." See Annette Becker, "The Great War: World War, Total War," *International Review of the Red Cross* 97 (2015): 1031.

3 The German jurist Franz von Liszt as quoted in Matthew Stibbe, "Civilian Internment and Civilian Internees in Europe, 1914–20," *Immigrants and Minorities* 26, nos. 1–2 (2008): 56.

4 The sheer scale and brutality of violence on the battlefield threw social relations into disarray. It also gave rise to a culture of war characterized by a heightened sense of grievance and animosity, which resulted in an intense hatred of the enemy and suspicion of outsiders. This suspicion was nurtured by sensationalist accounts of the enemy's brutality and duplicity. For a discussion of the impact of "war culture," see Matthew Stibbe, "Captivity, Forced Labour and Forced Migration during the First World War," *Immigrants and Minorities* 26, nos 1–2 (2008): 11–12.

5 Stibbe, "Civilian Internment and Civilian Internees in Europe," 55.

6 For a description of the role and purpose of internment camps in the colonies of South Africa and India at the turn of the century, see Aidan Forth, *Barbed-Wire Imperialism: Britain's Empire of Camps, 1876–1903* (Oakland: University of California Press, 2017), 43–99.

7 Ibid., 14.

8 A range of correspondence occurs between various parties with respect to the episode. See Hon. W.H. Walker, Acting Undersecretary of State for External Affairs, to Major General Wm. Otter, Director, Internment Operations, 12 August 1915; Lieutenant Colonel D. Macpherson, Staff Officer, Internment Operations, to Walker, 13 August 1915; Lieutenant Colonel E. Stanton, Secretary, Governor General of Canada, to Walker, 13 August 1915; Walker to Stanton, 14 August 1915; and Hon. G.E. Foster, Acting Undersecretary of State for External Affairs, to His Royal Highness the Governor General in Council, 25 August 1915. All in file 48-1, vol. 1156, RG 25 G1, LAC.

9 "Building on colonial precedents, World War I internment camps emerged out of a culture of confinement shared across the Western world. The Anglo-Boer War did not cause future episodes of concentration in any reductive sense. But it marked an important step in larger global developments: a 'guilt by association' logic, pioneered in South Africa, prevailed more and more in the age of 'total war,' as animosity extended from soldiers to civilians, who were reimagined as members of suspect collectivities. In this way, Britain's nineteenth-century empire of camps contributed to the erosion of earlier cultures of military captivity that had restricted internment solely to armed combatants." Forth, *Barbed-Wire Imperialism*, 219.

10 The legal opinion was submitted as a report to the Committee of the Privy Council. The tenets of the report were approved by the governor general on 28 August 1915 as PC 2039. See R. Boudreau, Clerk of the Privy Council, 28 August 1915, file 2616, vol. 819, RG 6 H1, LAC.

11 This rationale followed from the broad sentiment that held that those who were without work could be expected to cut wood or break stone in exchange for assistance. In the domestic setting, the popular work ethic of the "stonepile" had practical meaning, being seen as a remedy for vagrancy and

idleness. On wageless labour, poor relief, and the "stone-breaking" laws in late nineteenth-century Toronto, see Bryan D. Palmer and Gaetan Heroux, "'Cracking the Stone': The Long History of Capitalist Crisis and Toronto's Dispossessed, 1830–1930," *Labour/Le Travail* 69 (Spring 2012): 9–62.

12 Major General Wm. Otter to the Hon. C.J. Doherty, Minister of Justice, 3 November 1916, file 1633-1916, vol. 1929, RG 13 A2, LAC.

13 Ibid.

14 Deputy Minister of Justice E. Newcombe to Major General Wm. Otter, 22 November 1916, file 1633-1916, vol. 1929, RG 13 A2, LAC. Contrary to the statement, indigence was the most cited reason for arrest and internment. For examples of arrest records, see file Correspondence – Release of Prisoners, vol. 14, RG 117, LAC.

15 Brock Millman argues that enemy aliens were subjected to "an exceptionally repressive wartime judicial regime" that stemmed from the need to control residents of "doubtful allegiance." See Brock Millman, *Polarity, Patriotism, and Dissent in Great War Canada, 1914–1919* (Toronto: University of Toronto Press, 2016), 14.

16 Vernon Internment Camp, Internee Camp Committee, to the Governor General of Canada, 8 February 1919, file 422-42, vol. 233, RG 13 A2, LAC.

17 Suspicious and unusual occurrences were attributed to agents and saboteurs. As a result, private denunciations against suspect enemy aliens inundated the government and other officials. These ranged from the banal ("He is well off but has no visible means of support") to the ridiculous ("Must be a spy because he is a clever man who wears glasses and peddles books") to the completely outrageous ("He looks to be a German, and if not a German he at least owns a German Shepherd"). For but one example, see W.A. McCulloch to Colonel Young, Kingston, and the Officer Commanding Division III, 1 December 1914, file 26-3-12 (3), vol. 4413, RG 24, LAC.

18 In Alberta, large numbers of enemy aliens who had been arrested and then paroled in the early stages of the war failed to report even though there were consequences for not doing so. It was reported that their whereabouts could not be traced. See Laurence Fortescue, Royal North-West Mounted Police Comptroller, 26 November 1914, memorandum, file 1463, vol. 1150, RG 25 G1, LAC.

19 For a discussion of POW rights, see Richard Speed, *Prisoners, Diplomats, and the Great War: A Study in the Diplomacy of Captivity* (New York: Greenwood, 1990), 183–9. See also War Office (UK), Report on the Directorate of Prisoners of War, September 1920, file 15, vol. 1253, RG 25 G1, LAC.

20 Jones, "The Great War," 86–7.

21 Hon. Arthur Meighen, Solicitor General of Canada, to the Rt. Hon. Robert Borden, Prime Minister of Canada, 28 August 1914, reel C-4388, 105951, vol. 191, MG 26 H1(c), Robert Borden Papers, LAC.

22 *Edmonton Daily Bulletin*, 26 November 1914.

23 See, for example, Commissioner, Dominion Parks Branch, J.B. Harkin to F.H. Williamson, Deputy Commissioner, Dominion Parks Branch, 5 October 1915, file MR 176, vol. 190, RG 84, LAC; and J. Wardle to Major General Wm. Otter, Officer Commanding Internment Operations, 6 October 1915. See also John Black, Road Superintendent, to J.E. Griffith, Deputy Minister of Public Works, 28 and 29 April, file 1752, Okanagan District (1916), British Columbia Ministry of Transportation Records (hereafter BC Transportation Records).

24 John Anderson-Wilson interview, 4 May 1973, accn. no. 1838, Whyte Museum of the Canadian Rockies.

25 "Resolution Re: Employment of Interned Aliens to Construct Wagon Road from Nakusp to Hot Springs," n.d., file 1752, sec. 2, Okanagan District (1915), BC Transportation Records.

26 Major General Wm. Otter to the Officer Commanding 6th Division, Halifax, 13 July 1915; and Major H.F. Adams, Officer Commanding Halifax Internment Camp, to the Assistant Adjutant General, 6th Division, 15 July 1915. Both in file 73-1-6, vol. 4541, RG 24, LAC.

27 "Note on the Treatment of Enemy Aliens," 11 February 1918, reel C-3876, 1327-33, vol. 2, MG 30 E15, Loring Christie Papers, LAC.

28 J. Griffith, BC Deputy Minister of Public Works, to Lieutenant Colonel W. Ridgway-Wilson, BC Department of Alien Reservists, 1 February 1916, file 10/1917, vol. 1929, RG 13 A2, LAC.

29 J. Griffith to Major General Wm. Otter, 7 January 1916, file 1752, sec. 4, Okanagan District (1916), BC Transportation Records.

30 Regarding the interpretation of German imperial citizenship, see D.J. Hill, "Dual Citizenship in the German Imperial and State Citizenship Law," *American Journal of International Law* 12, no. 2 (1918): 356–63. In an age of imperialism, subjecthood was an idea shared with Britain. The notion was also implicitly understood in English-speaking Canada, where British imperial identity ran deep. Nevertheless, according to German authorities, despite being subjects of Germany, their status as civilians had to be respected.

31 Note Verbale, Berlin, 19 June 1916, file 15, part 2, vol. 1176, RG 25 G1, LAC; Note Verbale, Berlin, 28 July 1916, file: 1450–1470, vol. 205, RG 13 A2, LAC; Foreign Office diplomatic note, 19 August 1916, file: 1450–1470, vol. 205, RG 13 A2, LAC; Note Verbale, 4 August 1916, file "September 30 – October 30, 1916," vol. 1364, RG B8, LAC; Note Verbale, 28 May 1916, file "28 June – 31 August 1916," vol. 1369, RG B8, LAC; and Note Verbale, 22 January 1917, file "5 January – 21 February 1917," vol. 1369, RG B8, LAC. For a detailed account and assessment of German policy towards civilian prisoners and their use as forced labour, see Jens Thiel, "Between Recruitment and Forced Labour: The Radicalization of German Labour Policy in Occupied Belgium and Northern France," *First World War Studies* 4, no. 1 (2013): 39–50; and Christian Westerhoff, "'A Kind of Siberia': German Labour and Occupation Policies in Poland and Lithuania during the First World War," *First World War Studies* 4, no. 1 (2013): 53–63.

32 Note Verbale to the Embassy of the United States of America, 23 June 1915 and Bonar Law, Colonial Secretary to the Governor General, 5 and 12 July 1915. Both in file 48–1, vol. 1156, RG 25 G1, LAC.

33 G.E. Foster, Acting Undersecretary of State for External Affairs, to His Royal Highness the Governor General in Council, 25 August 1915, file 48–1, vol. 1156, RG 25 G1, LAC.

34 W.H. Walker, Acting Undersecretary of State for External Affairs to Major General Wm. Otter, 12 August 1915; Lieutenant Colonel D. Macpherson, Staff Officer, Internment Operations to W.H. Walker, 13 August 1915; Lieutenant Colonel E. Stanton, Secretary, Governor General of Canada, to W.H. Walker, 13 August 1915; and Walker to Stanton, 14 August 1915. All in file 48-1, vol. 1156, RG 25 G1, LAC.

35 Note Verbale, to the Embassy of the United States of America, 16 August 1915, file: 48–2, vol. 1157, RG 25 G1, LAC. A report on German allegations of abuses at the Amherst camp appeared in the *Montreal Star*, 23 August 1915 and the *New York Times*, 24 August 1915. Reports of conditions at the Nanaimo detention camp also appeared in the Seattle press, warranting a discussion about bringing in external observers who could counter some of the claims. See Joseph Pope, Undersecretary of State for External Affairs, to the Deputy Minister of Justice, E. Newcombe, 23 September 1915, file 48–2, vol. 1157, RG 25 G1, LAC.

36 "Reports have recently come to the knowledge of His Majesty's Government to the effect that the German Military Authorities had issued an order that certain classes of prisoners of war were henceforth to be treated with increased severity, this order having application more especially to His Majesty's Canadian troops." See Diplomatic note, Foreign Office to the United States Ambassador, 10 September 1915, LAC, reel C–4442, 16377, vol. 2884, MG 6 H1, Borden Papers, LAC.

Reprisals were a concern well into 1916, when, for example, German authorities complained about the abuses and the misdemeanours of guards as well as the forced labour of civilian prisoners at the Lethbridge and Banff camps. See Bonar Law, Colonial Secretary to the Governor General, 8 March 1916, file 1450–1470, vol. 205, RG 13 A2, LAC. For a report to the British Parliament on the issue of reprisals and the observations of the International Committee of the Red Cross during 1916, see "Correspondence with His Majesty's Minister at Berne respecting the Question of Reprisals against Prisoners of War," September 1916, file 15, pt. 2, vol. 1176, RG 25 G1, LAC.

37 Bonar Law, Colonial Secretary to the Governor General, 8 March 1916; and the Undersecretary of State for External Affairs, Joseph Pope, to the Minister of Interior, W.J. Roche, 29 March 1916. Both in file 1450–1470, vol. 205, RG 13 A2, LAC. For the statement of the Minster of Interior, W.J. Roche, see Canada, House of Commons, *Hansard*, 15 February 1916.

38 US Consul (Calgary) Harold Clum reported after inspecting the Banff internment camp: "If idle, they would only hurt themselves." See "Visit to Internment Camp at Banff, Alberta," 25 May 1916, file 3, vol. 4721, RG 24, LAC.

39 See, for example, Major General Otter to Joseph Pope, Undersecretary of State for External Affairs, 20 December 1915, file 48–2, vol. 1157, RG 25 G1, LAC.

40 F. Johnson, US Consul (Toronto) to the US Secretary of State, 11 May 1916; and Johnson to the US Secretary of State "Inspection of Fort Henry,"14 August 1916. Both in file 15, pt. 2, vol. 1176, RG 25 G1, LAC.

41 For Willrich's report, see G. Willrich, American Consul to the US Secretary of State, Washington, "Report on Conditions of German, Austro-Hungarian, Turkish and Bulgarian Subjects in Quebec Consular District and in the Detention Camp at Spirit Lake, Quebec," 29 December 1916, file 763.7115/2279, USNA.

For a detailed description of the conditions and situation at the Spirit Lake camp, see Peter Melnycky, "Badly Treated in Every Way: The Internment of Ukrainians in Quebec during the First World War," in *The Ukrainian Experience in Quebec*, ed. M. Diakowsky (Toronto: Basilian Press, 1994).

42 See, for example, Note Verbale, Berlin, 19 June 1916, file 15, pt. 2, vol. 1176, RG 25 G1, LAC; UK Foreign Office, Diplomatic note, 19 August 1916, file 1450–1470, vol. 205, RG 13 A2, LAC; Note Verbale, 4 August 1916, file "September 30 – October 30 1916," vol. 1364, RG B8, LAC; and Note Verbale, Berlin, 28 July 1916, file "28 June – 31 August 1916," vol. 1369, RG B8, LAC; and Note Verbale, 22 January 1917, file "5 January – 21 February 1917," vol. 1369, RG B8, LAC.

43 Heather Jones, "Goodbye to All That? Memory and Meaning in the Commemoration of the First World War," *Juncture* 20, no. 4 (2014): 290.

44 Brock Millman writes that, during the Great War, internment and other repressive mechanisms in Canada were "intended to satisfy British Canada, growing increasingly frantic as the burden of war was felt and disproportionately shouldered, [such] that the Borden government would do whatever had to be done to win the war, however drastic or distasteful." See Millman, *Polarity, Patriotism, and Dissent*,7–8.

45 See Jones, "The Great War," 85–9; and Stibbe, "Captivity, Forced Labour and Forced Migration," 10.

Chapter Four

1 William Katerberg, "The Irony of Identity: An Essay on Nativism, Liberal Democracy and Parochial Identities in Canada and the United States," *American Quarterly* 47, no. 3 (1995): 507.

2 On British imperial identity in Canada and how it conflates with Canadian nationalism at the turn of the century, see Douglas Cole, "The Problem of 'Nationalism' and 'Imperialism' in British Settlement Colonies," *Journal of British Studies* 10, no. 2 (1971): 160–82.

3 In his study of enemy alien treatment in Australia, Gerhard Fischer argues that the antagonism directed against the enemy alien was a continuation of the overseas fight at home. See G. Fischer, "Fighting the War at Home: The Campaign against Enemy Aliens in Australia during the First World War," in *Minorities in Wartime: National and Racial Groupings in Europe, North America, and Australia during the Two World Wars*, ed. Panikos Panayi (Oxford: Oxford University Press, 1993). For a discussion on British imperial identity and its effect on the martial spirit in Canada, see N. Smith, "Fighting the Alien Problem in a British Country: Returned Soldiers and Anti-Alien Activism in Wartime Canada, 1916–19," in *Other Combatants, Other Fronts: Competing Histories of the First World War*, ed. J.E. Kitchen, A. Miller, and L. Rowe (Newcastle, UK: Cambridge Scholars Publishing, 2011).

4 For an analytical assessment of the press and its agenda-setting role during crises, see Warwick Blood, "Agenda Setting: A Review of the Theory," *Media Information* 26, no. 1 (1982): 3–12.

5 On the global effect of British imperialism in shaping public attitudes towards enemy alien populations in the colonies, see Stefan Manz and Panikos Panayi, *Enemies in the Empire: Civilian Internment in the British Empire during the First World War* (Oxford: Oxford University Press, 2020).

6 See D. Welch, "War Aims and the 'Big Ideas' of 1914," in *Justifying War: Propaganda, Politics, and the Modern Age*, ed. D. Welch and Jo Fox (Basingstoke, UK: Palgrave, 2012).

7 The relationship between the metropole and colony is problematized by the role that overseas colonial elites play in the construction of empire. Still, as Douglas Cole argues, imperialism on the frontier is unsustainable without the core and centralizing idea of the metropole. Hence, the close identification with the "motherland" and imperialism's manifestation on the frontier as part of a wider "Britannic nationalism." See D. Cole, "Canada's 'Nationalistic' Imperialists," *Journal of Canadian Studies* 5, no. 3 (1970): 44–9. For a discussion of the interplay between colony and metropole and the need for more rigorous analysis of the dynamic between the two in the creation of imperial culture on the frontier, see R. Price, "One Big Thing: Britain, Its Empire and Their Imperial Culture," *Journal of British Studies* 45, no. 3 (July 2006): 502–27.

8 On the fragile nature of the imperial project and the need to constantly refurbish the idea on the frontier, see L. Colley, *Captives: Britain's Pursuit of Empire and How Its Soldiers and Civilians Were Held Captive by the Dream of Global Supremacy* (New York: Pantheon Books, 2002).

9 D. Cole, "The Problem of 'Nationalism' and Imperialism' in British Settlement Colonies," *Journal of British Studies* 10, no. 2 (1971): 171–4.

10 The seamless integration of Germans into the dominant settler society before the war as merchants and professionals reinforced this understanding. Admiration for German culture and the Anglo-Canadian majority's social acceptance of Germans is explored in P. Moogk, "Uncovering the

Enemy Within: British Columbians and the German Menace," *BC Studies* 182 (Summer 2014): 50–2.

11 *Vancouver Daily Province*, 3 and 8 August 1914. Editorials ruminating on the possibility of a German invasion launched from the United States persisted well into 1915. See *Vancouver Sun*, 5, 15 January and 13 February 1915.

12 *Vancouver Sun*, 19 August 1914; and *Daily Herald* (Nanaimo), 18 September 1914.

13 *Vancouver Sun*, 10 September 1914.

14 *Daily Herald* (Nanaimo), 25 October 1914; and *Pioneer* (Phoenix, BC), 3 October 1914.

15 *Daily Colonist* (Victoria), 5 December 1914.

16 "Fully two hundred Russians [Ruthenians] were found in various tenements today so weak from sheer starvation that they were unable to leave their bunks. They had eaten no food for several days being unemployed. The authorities are providing food and will put the men to work as soon as they are able." *Free Press* (Nanaimo), 15 May 1915.

17 *Vancouver Sun*, 8 April 1915.

18 Ibid., 17 February 1915; and *Vancouver Daily Province*, 29 April 1915.

19 *Vancouver Daily Province*, 21 May 1915. Rumours of alleged celebrations in German communities across Canada regarding the sinking were variously reported. See, for example, *Kelowna Record*, 20 May 1915.

20 For an account of the riot, see T. Raynolds, "A Case Study in Attitudes towards Enemy Aliens in British Columbia, 1914–1919" (MA thesis, University of British Columbia, April 1973), 63–9.

21 See, for example, *Vancouver Sun*, 11 and 12 May 1915. In addition to the boycott, a proposal before the district council of North Vancouver argued that the sale of land by or to enemy aliens should be prohibited "for the reason that the money from such sales might be used to assist the enemy." *Vancouver Sun*, 18 May 1915.

22 *Vancouver Sun*, 10 May 1915.

23 Ibid., 12 May 1915.

24 *Daily Colonist* (Victoria), 14 May 1915.

25 *Vancouver Sun*, 21 May 1915.

26 See editorials, *Vancouver Sun*, 17, 18, 19, 20, 21, 22, and 23 May 1915.

27 *Vancouver Sun*, 13 May 1915. For a similar expression of concern, see *Free Press* (Nanaimo), 14 May 1915.

28 Corporate concern over the economic effects of widespread enemy alien job dismissals led to some nervous resistance. The CPR western superintendent assured the readers of the *Vancouver World* that unnaturalized enemy aliens were being "weeded out" but in fairness to those who were naturalized, "where employees had lived up to the best tradition of British citizenship, and had given the company good service, it [was against] British fair play or common justice to discharge them." *Vancouver World*, 17 June 1915.

29 For a comprehensive discussion of the politics of the labour situation and internment as it unfolded in Fernie, BC, see W. Norton, *Fernie at War, 1914–1919* (Halfmoon Bay, BC: Caitlin Press, 2017), 51–72.

30 *District Ledger*, 12 June 1915. See also *Daily News* (Nelson), 9 June 1915.

31 *Vancouver World*, 10 June 1915.

32 *Vancouver Sun*, 18 June1915.

33 *District Ledger*, 10 July 1915.

34 The value of work to be undertaken by interned enemy aliens was reported at $1.5 million per year. It was noted: "Although it costs a good deal to maintain the internment camps, there will be, therefore, a large amount of valuable work accomplished to show for the expenditure which was itself unavoidable." See *Crossfield Chronicle*, 31 December 1915.

When the decision was taken to shut down the original Monashee camp because of supply problems, provincial conservatives who were closely aligned with local business interests demanded the road not be abandoned. The argument was made that the road "would quickly justify its construction in increased revenue." But, more to the point, "an opportunity to build this road probably would never occur again." Under pressure, the Internment Directorate would authorize the creation of the Edgewood camp to complete the road. See *Daily News* (Nelson), 28 September 1915.

35 *Vernon News*, 27 May 1915. As a facility dedicated to the internment of so-called first-class prisoners – POWs of an "officer class" – the administration of the Vernon camp was consistently criticized for its benign attitude towards the prisoners held there. See, for example, *Omineca Miner* (Hazelton, BC), 28 August 1918.

36 *Vancouver Sun*, 29 May 1915.

37 Ibid., 23 June 1915.

38 On some of the incidents reported, see *Daily Colonist* (Victoria), 5 June 1915; *Vernon News*, 16 December 1915.

39 *Vernon News*, 19 October 1916; and *Vancouver World*, 16 September 1916.

40 *Vancouver Sun*, 7 December 1915.

41 *Daily Colonist* (Victoria), 12 December 1916.

42 *Vancouver Sun*, 11 and 13 September 1916.

43 Ibid. 20, 21, and 23 November 1916.

44 Ibid., 6 February 1917.

45 *Daily Colonist* (Victoria), 7 April 1918.

46 See *Abbotsford Post*, 30 May 1918.

47 For example, *Vancouver Sun*, 14, 15, 16, 18 November 1917 and 6 January 1919. An account of a captured Canadian soldier crucified by German troops was also widely circulated at this time. An example of the story appears in the *Free Press* (Nanaimo), 12 May 1915.

48 *Vancouver Sun*, 14 November 1918.

49 *Vancouver World*, 27 September 1918.

50 *Kelowna Record*, 28 August 1919.
51 *Daily Colonist* (Victoria), 17 December 1918.
52 *Vancouver Sun*, 28 February 1919; and *Daily Colonist* (Victoria), 28 February 1919.
53 *Vancouver Sun*, 25 March 1919.
54 *Kelowna Record*, 13 February 1919.
55 *Daily Colonist* (Victoria), 8 February 1919.
56 *Vancouver Sun*, 1 February 1919.
57 Ibid., 12 February 1919.
58 On political deportation at this time, see B. Roberts, *Whence They Came: Deportation from Canada, 1900–1935* (Ottawa: University of Ottawa Press, 1988), chap. 5. The arrest and internment of political activists is also described in G. Kealey, "State Repression of Labour and the Left in Canada 1914–20: The Impact of the First World War," *Canadian Historical Review* 73, no. 3 (1992): 300–3.
59 *Vancouver Sun*, 5 February 1919.
60 *Kelowna Record*, 13 and 20 November 1919; and *Vancouver World*, 13 November 1919. See also the incident reported in the *Okanagan Commoner* that described how, upon returning to Penticton, a prominent businessman of enemy origin was accosted and compelled to kneel in muck and kiss the Union Jack. He was forced to leave the district but not before being told that "all other Germans trying to come back to this part of Canada would meet with similar treatment." *Okanagan Commoner*, 20 March 1919.
61 *Vancouver Sun*, 2 May 1919
62 Ibid., 19 May 1915.

Chapter Five

A variant of this text was originally published as "'Enemies of Our Country': Internment in Canada's Rocky Mountains National Park, 1915–1917," in *Out of Line, Out of Place: A Global and Local History of World War I Internments*, ed. R. Kowner and I. Rachamimov (Ithaca, NY: Cornell University Press, 2022).
1 Canada, *Hansard* (House of Commons Debates), 15 February 1916, 850.
2 Ibid.
3 Unemployment was the key issue identified with the enemy alien, and internment was seen as a viable solution. Calgary's mayor, Michael Costello, increasingly concerned by the problem that enemy alien joblessness poased, conceded internment was necessary and even vital. Without work, their presence was a liability. Internment, he posited, was the only practical option since "there was no way out of the dilemma." *Calgary Daily Herald*, 14 February 1915.
4 Internment was introduced to detain those enemy reservists who were inclined to return to their respective homelands to join the colours. In the

early stages of the war, Canada followed Britain's lead that reservists be detained, although this position was modified by selectively interning those who crossed the US-Canada border.

5 F.H. Williamson, Deputy Commissioner, Dominion Parks Branch, to W. Cory, Deputy Minister, Department of Interior, "Memorandum: Regarding the Employment of German and Austrian Prisoners in the Dominion Parks," 28 October 1914, file 1639–59, vol. 189, RG 13 A2, LAC.

6 Canada, Department of the Interior, *Report of the Commissioner of Dominion Parks* (Ottawa: King's Printer, 1916), 11.

7 E.J. Hart, *J.B. Harkin: Father of Canada's National Parks* (Edmonton: University of Alberta Press, 2010), 119.

8 B. Waiser, *Park Prisoners: The Untold Story of Canada's National Parks, 1915–1946* (Saskatoon: Fifth House, 1995), 12. Bennett's insistence that the prisoners were not to be coddled, however, ran contrary to the convention regarding war prisoners, with which Canadian government officials would have been familiar. See Colonial Secretary to the Governor General, and referred to E. Newcombe, Deputy Minister of Justice, "Special treatment to certain classes of interned enemy subjects," 2 March 1915, file 117–36, vol. 190, RG 13 A2, LAC.

9 *Crag and Canyon* (Banff, AB), 19 June 1915. There was some initial speculation that two camps would be created, one to be situated on the flats near Castle Mountain and the other nearby, but the idea would be abandoned. See *Crag and Canyon*, 26 June 1915. The setup of the camp is described in a daily diary kept by camp officials. This diary is reproduced in its entirety in Bohdan S. Kordan and Peter J. Melnycky, eds, *In the Shadow of the Rockies: The Diary of the Castle Mountain Camp, 1915–1917* (Edmonton: CIUS Press, 1991).

10 Officer Commanding Castle Internment Camp to Officer Commanding Military District No. 13, 23 July 1915, file 3, vol. 4729, RG 24, LAC.

11 *Calgary Daily Herald*, 29 July 1915.

12 The protocol on captured combatants made a distinction between officers and enlisted men. For civilian prisoners, this translated into the difference between men of property and those without means. Following the rule issued by the Colonial Office, the distinction entitled men of a "superior class" to forgo work and be entitled to better messing and accommodations. See "Accommodation. Officers, Prisoners of War," Officer Commanding Internment Operations to Officer Commanding Military District No. 13 (Alberta), 18 February 1915, file 448–14–20 (1), vol. 4694, RG 24, LAC.

13 *Crag and Canyon*, 12 June 1915.

14 Officer Commanding Castle Internment Camp to Officer Commanding Military District 13, 23 July 1915, file 3, vol. 4729, RG 24, LAC.

15 *Crag and Canyon*, 24 and 31 July and 4 August 4, 1915.

16 Major Duncan Stuart to Officer Commanding Military District No. 13, 4 November 1915, file 3, vol. 4729, RG 24, LAC; and Officer Commanding Military District No. 13 (Alberta) to Major-General Otter, 5 November 1915, file 533–51, vol. 201, RG 13 A2, LAC. On the escapes, see "Report of Prisoners of

War Escaped from Internment Camp, Castle Alta.," October 1915, file 3, vol. 4729, RG 24, LAC.

17 *Rabochyi narod* (Winnipeg), no. 31, 28 October 1915.

18 Letter of N. Olinyk, n.d., file 3, vol. 4729, RG 24, LAC.

19 "Comparative Statement Showing Caloric Value of Canadian Ration Based on Seven Days Issue for Non-Working Group," n.d., file 1–1–1918/13, vol. 3413, RG 25, LAC; Major Duncan Stuart, Officer Commanding Castle Mountain Internment Camp, to Officer Commanding Military District No. 13 (Alberta), 13 September 1915, file 3, vol. 4729, RG 24, LAC; and "Maintenance of Discipline Among Prisoners of War," n.d., file 34–13 (4), vol. 4280, RG 24, LAC.

20 Waiser, *Park Prisoners*, 21.

21 Ibid.

22 *Crag and Canyon*, 5 February 1916; and *Calgary Daily Herald*, 7, 9, and 23 February 1916. See also P.W. Lackenbauer, "The Military and 'Mob Rule': The CEF Riots in Calgary, 1916" *Canadian Military History* 10, no. 1 (2001): 31–43.

23 Private George Lomax to Brigadier General E. Cruickshank, 22 April 1916, file 2, vol. 4721, RG 24, LAC. Private Lomax's wish was granted. He was killed on the Western Front a year later.

24 *Crag and Canyon*, 22 April 1916.

25 Jacob Kondro to Brigadier General E.A. Cruikshank, 8 February 1916, file 2, vol. 4721, RG 24, LAC. For a complete description of the Kondro case, see Kordan and Melnycky, *In the Shadow of the Rockies*, 6.

26 The Spray River Road project was described in the Parks Branch's annual report as "one of the most important public works undertaken by the department" in so far as it promised to be "one of the most popular drives in the locality." See *Annual Report of the Department of the Interior for the Fiscal Year Ending March 31, 1917* (Ottawa: King's Printer, 1918).

27 Note Verbale to the Embassy of the United States of America, 23 June 1915 and Bonar Law, Colonial Secretary, to the Governor General of Canada, 5 and 12 July 1915. All in file 48–1, vol. 1156, RG 25 G1, LAC.

28 H. Clum, US Consul (Calgary), 25 May 1916, file 3, vol. 4721, RG 24, LAC.

29 "Prisoners of War Camp at Banff," 29 June 1916, FO 383/239, Foreign Office Papers, United Kingdom National Archives, hereafter UKNA.

30 Major General Wm. Otter to Major Peter Spence, 22 June 1916; and Major General Otter to Brigadier General E. Cruickshank, 22 June 1916. Both in FO 383/239, Foreign Office Papers, UKNA.

31 Waiser, *Park Prisoners*, 30.

32 *Annual Report of Surveys and Construction of Highways in the Dominion Parks, 1915* (Ottawa: King's Printer, 1915).

33 *Annual Report of Surveys and Construction of Highways in the Dominion Parks, 1916* (Ottawa: King's Printer, 1916).

34 Canada, Sessional Paper No. 25, "Dominion Parks," 1917, 5.

35 *Crag and Canyon*, 2 September 1916.

36 Major Spence to Brigadier General E. Cruickshank, 12 December 1916; and Major Peter Spence to Brigadier General E. Cruickshank, 27 April 1916. Both in file 3422 (1), vol. 757, RG 6 H1, LAC.

37 Regarding the Perchaliuk case, see Major Spence to the Assistant Adjutant General, 9 December 1916; Assistant Adjutant General to Major Spence, 11 December 1916; and Major Spence to the Assistant Adjutant General, 20 December 1916. All in file 3, vol. 4729/1, RG 24, LAC.

38 On the Konowalczuk shooting, see Board of Inquiry, 21 August 1916, file 2, vol. 4728, RG 24, LAC; and *Crag and Canyon*, 19 August 1916.

39 *Crag and Canyon*, 18 November 1916.

40 Ibid.

41 Ibid., 23 December 1916.

42 Ibid., 30 December 1916.

43 *Annual Report of the Department of the Interior for the Fiscal Year Ending March 31, 1917* (Ottawa: King's Printer, 1918). See also Waiser, *Park Prisoners*, 43.

44 Individual prisoners were identified based on their behavior while interned, and this was cited in a prepared list. See, for example, "Supplementary List of Prisoners at Banff, Alta.," 23 April 1917, file 3326 (3), vol. 757, RG 6 H1, LAC.

45 For a discussion of the project, see file R313, vol. 70, RG 84, LAC. See also *Crag and Canyon*, 7 April and 26 May 1917.

Chapter Six

A variant of this text was originally published as Bohdan S. Kordan, "Internment in Ontario's Northland," *Ontario History* 113, no. 1 (2021): 54–79.

1 Watson Kirkconnell, "Kapuskasing: An Historical Sketch," *Bulletin of the Departments of History and Political and Economic Science in Queen's University* 38 (January 1921); and Captain F.W. Kirkconnell, "When We First Locked Up Fritz: The First Authentic Story of Our Internment Camps," *Maclean's*, 1 September 1920.

Descriptions, in passing, of internment at Kapuskasing include Desmond Morton, "Sir William Otter and Internment Operations in Canada during the First World War," *Canadian Historical Review* 55, no. 1 (1974): 32–58; Desmond Morton, *The Canadian General: Sir William Otter* (Toronto: Hakkert, 1974); and Dieter Buse and Graeme Mount, *Untold: Northeastern Ontario's Military Past* (Sudbury, ON: Latitude 46 Publishing, 2018). More recently, the correspondence of Adolph Hundt and the memoir of John Boychuk, internees held at Kapuskasing, have been retold in different formats. See Dominique Villeneuve, *Heritage by Default, 1914–1920*, trans. Melanie Lalonde (Kapuskasing, ON: n.p. 2014); and Kassandra Luciuk and Nicole Marie Burton, *Enemy Alien: A True Story of Life behind Barbed Wire* (Toronto: Between the Lines, 2020).

2 *Manitoba Free Press*, 10 December 1914. See also *Toronto Daily Star*, 10 December 1914; *Sault Star*, 11 December 1914; and *Ottawa Citizen*, 11 December 1914.
3 Hon. W.H. Hearst to J.F. Whitson, 11 December 1914, reel MS 5542, "Kapuskasing Detention Camp Re: Clearing Land," RG 14-157, Archives of Ontario (hereafter AO).
4 Felix Johnson, US Consul, to the Secretary of State, Washington, 11 December 1914, file 763.72115.345, Department of State Records, USNA.
5 Commissioner J.F. Whitson, Northern Development Branch, to G.H. Grisdale, Director of Experimental Farms, Ottawa, 25 March 1915, reel MS 5542, "Kapuskasing Detention Camp Re: Sawmill," RG 14-157, AO.
6 *Empire and Mail* (Toronto), 6 August 1915; and *Empire and Mail*, 10 August 1915.
7 Note Verbale to the Embassy of the United States of America, 23 June 1915, file 48-1, vol. 1156, RG 25 G1, LAC.
8 On public perception, see, for example, *Ottawa Journal*, 11 December 1914.
9 The deputy minister of justice, E. Newcombe, first articulated this position, which would be submitted in a report to the Committee of the Privy Council. See R. Boudreau, Clerk of the Privy Council, 28 August 1915, file 2616, vol. 819, RG 6 H1, LAC.
10 *Montreal Gazette*, 15 January 1915.
11 J.F. Whitson, Commissioner, Northern Development Branch, to J.A. Stewart, Inspector, 14 March 1916, reel MS 5542, "Kapuskasing Detention Camp, Re: a/c for Board," RG 14-157, AO.
12 Numerous reports and correspondence detailed both the quality of the recruits and the problems encountered. See, for example, "Recruits A.M.C. at Kapuskasing," 28 November 1915, file 34-1-3 (10), vol. 4279, RG 24, LAC; "10th Royal Grenadier Detachment Doing Duty at Kapuskasing," 9 December 1915, file 34-1-3 (11), file 34-1-3 (11), vol. 4279, RG 24, LAC; and Officer Commanding Kapuskasing Internment Camp to the A.A.G., 2nd Military Division, 10 December 1915, file 34-1-3 (II), vol. 4279, RG 24, LAC.
13 Major General Wm. Otter, Officer Commanding Internment Operations, to Brigadier General E. Cruickshank, Officer Commanding Military District No.13, 16 December 1915, file 448-14-20, vol. 4695, RG 24, LAC.
14 Lieutenant Colonel G. Royce, Officer Commanding Kapuskasing Internment Camp, to the A.A.G., 2nd Military Division, Exhibition Camp, Toronto, 7 February 1916, file 34-6-11 (1), vol. 4360, RG 24, LAC.
15 For examples of monthly accounts, see: "Kapuskasing Detention Camp, Re: a/c for Board," March–June 1916, reel MS 5542, RG 14-157, AO.
16 Lieutenant Colonel G. Royce, Officer Commanding Kapuskasing Internment Camp, to the A.A.G., 2nd Military Division, Exhibition Camp, Toronto, 20 March 1916, file 34-6-11 (1), vol. 4360, RG 24, LAC.
17 *Globe* (Toronto), 19 February 1916.
18 Lieutenant Colonel G. Royce, Officer Commanding Kapuskasing Internment Camp, to the A.A.G., 2nd Military Division, 20 March 1916, file 34-6-11 (1), vol. 4360, RG 24, LAC.

19 Royce to the A.A.G., 2nd Military Division, 16 March 1916, file 34-6-11 (1), vol. 4360, RG 24, LAC.

20 Professor D. Morton refers to the list of injuries and infirmary records at Kapuskasing. See Morton, "Sir William Otter," 47.

21 The prisoner riot was extensively covered in several dailies, including the *Globe* (Toronto), 16 and 17 May 1916. On official reports, see Major General Otter, Officer Commanding Internment Operations, to Brigadier General W. Logie, District Officer Commanding 2nd Military Division, 13 May 1916; and Brigadier General W. Logie to the Hon. Sam Hughes, Militia Headquarters, 13 May 1916. Both in file: 34-6-11 (1), vol. 4360, RG 24, LAC. And see "Report of Riot of Prisoners of War," 12 May 1916, file 763.72115.2127, Department of State Records, USNA.

22 Lieutenant Colonel G. Royce, Officer Commanding Kapuskasing Internment Camp, to Brigadier General W. Logie, Officer Commanding 2nd Military Division, 19 May 1916, file 34-6-11 (1), vol. 4360, RG 24, LAC.

23 Major General Wm. Otter, General Officer Commanding Internment Operations, to Brigadier General W.A. Logie, Officer Commanding 2nd Military District, 25 May 1916, file 34-6-11 (1), vol. 4360, RG 24, LAC.

24 See *Globe* (Toronto), 15 April 1916; and *Sault Star*, 15 April 1916.

25 Bonar Law, UK Colonial Secretary, to the Governor General, 5 and 12 July 1915, file 48-1, vol. 1156, RG 25 G1, LAC.

26 See the discussion in Stefan Manz and Panikos Panayi, *Enemies in the Empire: Civilian Internment in the British Empire during the First World War* (Oxford: Oxford University Press, 2020).

27 *Pembroke Standard*, 20 May 1917.

28 Major General Wm. Otter to the Minister of Justice, Hon. C.J. Doherty, 24 February and 1 March 1917, file 1633-1916, vol. 1929, RG 13 A2, LAC. The episode is also described in Morton, "Sir William Otter," 50.

29 Major General Wm. Otter, General Officer Commanding Internment Operations, to Captain W.R. Creighton, Assistant Private Secretary, Minister of the Militia, 26 September 1917, file 5251, vol. 765, RG 6, LAC.

30 "I decided to call their bluff right there and then. I called for about twelve men, posted armed sentries over the other bunkhouses, in case their inmates attempted a mix-up, went into No. 1 [bunkhouse] with Capts. Gibson and Kirkconnell and ordered the prisoners up for roll call. A few hesitated, but an automatic six-shooter poked in their faces made them step lively. They stood up like sheep and answered their names. Afterwards, I had them counted, then told [Prisoner] Baffin to roll his blankets and come out, which he did most obediently. Furthermore, I told [Prisoner] No. 2232 Policardo to follow suit, seeing he was so mouthy just previously. He came like a child. After we left there was not a sound in No. 1, and the whole thing was done so quietly, and they cowed down so completely." See Officer Commanding Kapuskasing Internment Camp, Lieutenant Colonel W. E. Date, to Major General Wm. Otter, 1 October 1917, file 5330, vol. 765, RG 6 H1, LAC.

31 "These men have absolutely refused to saw any wood to keep themselves warm. There is a big stove in the building, wood at the door, saw and saw-horse, but they say 'they will freeze in hell before cutting wood.' If they want to freeze, it's their outlook. Troops will not be allowed to cut their wood." See Lieutenant Colonel W.E. Date to Major General Wm. Otter, 5 October 1917, file 5330, vol. 765, RG 6 H1, LAC.

32 B.R. Iseli, Consul General of Switzerland, to Swiss Legation, London, England, 22 September 1917; B.R. Iseli to Major General Wm. Otter, Director Internment Operations, 24 September 1917; B.R. Iseli to Lieutenant Colonel W.E. Date, Officer Commanding Kapuskasing Internment Camp, 10 October 1917; and Date to Iseli, 19 October 1917. All in file 5330, vol. 765, RG 6 H1, LAC.

33 Lieutenant Colonel W.E. Date to Major General Wm. Otter, 21 August 1917, file 5330, vol. 764, RG 6 H1, LAC.

34 Lieutenant Colonel W.E. Date to Staff Officer, Internment Operations, 4 November 1917, file 5175, vol. 765, RG 6 H1, LAC.

35 The internees complained: "Though the letter of International Agreement relating to the treatment of prisoners might be adhered to verbally, the interpretation is of such a spirit of malevolence and petty annoyance which makes life almost unbearable." See "Officers Interned at Kapuskasing" to B.R. Iseli, Consul General of Switzerland, 11 October 1917, file 4178, vol. 760, RG 6 H1, LAC.

36 Lieutenant Colonel W.E. Date to Staff Officer, Internment Operations, 16 November 1917, file 5330, vol. 764, RG 6 H1, LAC.

37 Lieutenant Colonel W.E. Date to Major General Wm. Otter, 4 November 1917, file 5330, vol. 764, RG 6 H1, LAC. For a first-hand account of the strike, see Kirkconnell, "When We First Locked Up Fritz."

38 A senior officer of the General Staff, 2nd Military Division (Toronto), conducted the investigation. For a copy of the report, see "Report on Kapuskasing – Saturday February 9th, 1918," file 34-6-11 (3), vol. 4360, RG 24, LAC. The complaints and allegations lodged against Lieutenant Colonel W.E. Date are found in file 5251, vol. 765, RG 6 H1, LAC.

39 Untitled document, n.d., 54130–1, reel C-4331, vol. 100, MG 26 H1, Robert Borden Papers, LAC. See also "Alien Labour, 16 February 1918," 53424–4326, reel C-4331, vol. 100, MG 26 H1, Robert Borden Papers, LAC.

40 See E. Newcombe, Deputy Minister of Justice, to Major General Otter, Director, Internment Operations, 14 May 1919, file 6712 (2), vol. 770, RG 6 H1, LAC.

41 As an ancillary aspect of internment, the role that deportation would play in ridding the country of those deemed "undesirable" is explored by Barbara Roberts, *Whence They Came: Deportation from Canada, 1900–1935* (Ottawa: University of Ottawa Press 1988), chaps. 2 and 3.

42 "Repatriation of Prisoners of War," Major General Wm. Otter to the Minister of Justice, 23 August 1919, file 1490-150, vol. 237, RG 13 A1, LAC.

43 At the height of the troubles, one hundred labour activists were identified for deportation – thirty-six of them from Winnipeg. To this number were added other radicals. See Donald Avery, *"Dangerous Foreigners": European Immigrant Workers and Labour Radicalism in Canada, 1896–1932* (Toronto: McClelland and Stewart, 1983), 85; and Donald Avery, *Reluctant Host: Canada's Response to Immigrant Workers, 1896–1994* (Toronto: McClelland and Stewart, 1994), 79. The arrests in Alberta are described in Howard Palmer, *Patterns of Prejudice: A History of Nativism in Alberta* (Toronto: McClelland and Stewart, 1983), 55.

44 Lieutenant Colonel W.E. Date to Major General Wm. Otter, 12 May 1919, file 6712 (2), vol. 770, RG 6 H1, LAC. Information regarding the deportation of militants was shared by Date with a Toronto newspaper. See "More Reds Are Still to Go," *Empire and Mail* (Toronto), 20 January 1920.

45 Letter of "First Class POWs" to Major General Otter, Director, Internment Operations, 11 August 1919, file 6712 (3), vol. 770, RG 6 H1, LAC.

46 Captain F.W. Kirkconnell, Officer Commanding Pretorian Party, to the Staff Officer, Internment Operations, "Prisoners Repatriated per SS Pretorian," 21 September 1919, file 6712 (4), vol. 770, RG 6 H1, LAC.

47 See the discussion in "Resolution to the Executive Council of Canada," n.d., 53439–44, reel C-4331, vol. 99, MG 26 H1, Robert Borden Papers, LAC.

48 Kirkconnell, "Kapuskasing," 13–5.

Epilogue

A variant of this text was delivered as a keynote address on 8 August 1993 on Ukrainian Heritage Day at the Ukrainian Cultural Heritage Village, a government of Alberta provincial historic site, and published as Bohdan S. Kordan, "Righting Historical Wrongs: Internment, Acknowledgment and Redress," *Canadian Speeches: Issues of the Day* 8, no. 5 (1993): 2–6. The address presages the passage of the Internment of Persons of Ukrainian Origin Recognition Act, 25 November 2005, which required the government of Canada to recognize First World War internment as a historical wrong and to provide funding for educational projects. The Canadian First World War Internment Recognition Fund was established for this purpose on 9 May 2008.

1 Canada, *Hansard* (House of Commons Debates), 22 September 1988.

2 The Hon. Jean Charest, minister of the environment at the time, whose cabinet duties included responsibility for the national parks, accepted the findings of the National Historic Sites and Monuments Board, which dismissed First World War internment as "not, in and of itself, of national historic significance." See *Edmonton Journal*, 31 March and 2, 12, 13 April 1993; and *Toronto Star*, 4 May 1993.

3 Remarks of Conservative Mississauga-South MP Don Blenkarn as quoted in *Alberta Report*, 17 December 1990.

4 Debating redress, the Reform MP for Swift Current-Maple Creek, Lee Morrison, would ask: "Why is that the descendants of these Ukrainian settlers have their hands out now. I suspect that it is because they see everyone else lining up for grants." Canada, *Hansard* (House of Commons), 18 October 1994.

INDEX